MAKING REAGAN

A MEMOIR FROM THE PRODUCER OF THE REAGAN MOVIE

MARK JOSEPH

BP
BOOKS

PRAISE FOR MAKING REAGAN

"Mark Joseph's *Making REAGAN* relates the challenges of making a movie of one of America's most beloved presidents. Joseph takes us step by step into the fascinating aspects of research into Reagan's life. His journey to making a memorable film sends you to his search for a writer, film financing, director, talent and distributor and demonstrates remarkable dedication to his project. This is a must read for all Americans."

—**Howard Kazanjian**, Producer, *Star Wars, Return of The Jedi, Raiders of the Lost Ark*

"Movies are hard to make, and people can be hard to fully understand. In *Making REAGAN*, Mark Joseph takes us on two journeys: the long and winding road of making a major motion picture and one of understanding as he tries to dig beneath the surface and find out who the real Ronald Reagan was and what we can learn from him."

—**Dr. Phil McGraw**

"Mark Joseph returned Hollywood to the classic stream of American filmmaking with his biopic of the fiercely anti-communist Ronald Reagan, a carefully edited, beautifully musical love story surrounding the near-apocalyptic struggle between the free world and the totalitarian hell of the USSR. In *Making REAGAN* he takes the reader behind the scenes of his two-decade odyssey, bringing the story to the silver screen."

   —Dr. Jordan Peterson

"Movies are hard to make. I know. I've been in 152 of them. But imagine making a movie in the middle of a pandemic, being forced to shut down twice, waiting for an actor's strike to end and then waiting until people felt comfortable going to theaters again. That's what Mark and I endured. I measure my feelings for a movie by how I felt when I was making it, and that makes Reagan the favorite of my career thus far. If you liked the movie, I think you'll really enjoy this story of how it came to be."

   —Dennis Quaid

"Mark Joseph's quest to recreate the very essence of President Ronald Reagan was remarkable, daunting, and brilliant. Journey alongside Joseph and come to know more deeply the heart of the man the whole world respected and loved."

   —Karen Kingsbury

"Ronald Reagan was the ultimate all American. He was motivated by his strong faith and firm convictions. In *Making REAGAN,* Mark Joseph chronicles his arduous journey of bringing REAGAN to the silver screen. Going from athlete, to successful actor, to the President of the United States (leader of the free world) is an astounding feat. Getting any movie made is a daunting undertaking. Progressing from a good idea to your local movie theatre is a journey in itself. So many things have to happen correctly for that film to be made. Casting Dennis Quaid was genius. Mark Joseph, with his fascinating backstory, could make another movie about getting Reagan made. Presidents are always well regarded after they are gone. While in office they are either the hero or the villain. A fascinating read about a fascinating man."

   —Alice Cooper

"'Mr. Gorbachev, tear down this wall!' Ronald Reagan was the great communicator. A complex man who marched to the beat of his own drum. Not widely known is that he started off as a Democrat and then switched to the Republican Party. REAGAN, the motion picture, needed to come out in these very politically divisive times. And now with the book *Making REAGAN*, perhaps people on both sides of the aisle will more fully understand why Ronald Reagan was the right president for the right time."

   —Gene Simmons, KISS

"Mark Joseph and his team have done a remarkable job to present a film that is historically accurate and entertaining. This is the story of the effort to tell that remarkable story."

   —Edwin Meese III

For Jordan

CONTENTS

FOREWORD

When I traveled to the Reagan Ranch to interview Dennis Quaid about his playing Ronald Reagan in a movie, I had no idea of the journey that was ahead for the film and its filmmakers. Watching that process evolve over six years, through a pandemic and an actor's strike, gave me a new appreciation for the work that goes into making a film.

Through it all, Mark Joseph and his team persevered, leaving me stunned in my seat, and in awe, as I watched the final product. I told my audience afterward: "Run, don't walk, to see this movie." The experience was breathtaking.

Now, with *Making REAGAN*, Mark takes us behind the scenes of the two decades he spent not only making this movie, but also trying to understand Ronald Reagan—whose own biographer declared him to be "inscrutable." Not for Mark who, in *Making REAGAN,* gives us a full sense of the man—who he was and what he believed.

I know you'll enjoy this book as an enriching companion to this amazing film. With any luck, the lessons to be learned can help us avoid making the same mistakes as happened to those who crossed Reagan, and maybe help save the West in the process.

—Megyn Kelly, *New York Times* bestselling author and journalist.

1

WHERE GREATNESS COMES FROM

My wife, four daughters, and I were driving a rented minivan from Chicago to St. Louis for my cousin's wedding when I suddenly became aware of a police car behind me with flashing lights, signaling me to pull over to the shoulder of the road. A clean cut, very young and very nice police officer looking to be in his early twenties approached my window and asked me if I realized I had been driving in a construction zone where the speed limit was 45.

I told him I could swear the sign had just said 65. He acknowledged that the speed limit was 65 awhile back, but it had most recently been 45. It wasn't until later that I figured out I was the latest victim of a speed trap, and I would be charged with driving 20 miles over the speed limit.

As the officer filled out the ticket, I noticed his hands were shaking. Must be new on the job, I figured, and sensing his weakness, I tried to see if he wouldn't let me off with a warning. He said he couldn't and noted I must appear in court in a month.

"But I'm visiting from California," I pleaded. "There's no way I can come back in a month."

He urged me to call the court and see if they would speed up my court appearance. It was only then, as he finished writing the ticket, that I looked at it and noticed the jurisdiction in which my "crime" has been committed was Dixon, Illinois, the hometown of Ronald Reagan.

As I tried to process this information, I was reminded of what my mother, who was just as devout as Reagan's mother, often said, that there is a Divine Plan, and that nothing is random in a universe where God orders the steps of His children. Which in my case meant that I was being led to Dixon, against my will, for a reason.

But I still had details to attend to: Following the officer's suggestion, I pulled over and called a clerk at Dixon City Hall to explain my predicament. She agreed I could come and see the judge—but not until the next day. So, I announced to the family, we were spending the night in Dixon, Illinois.

We exited the highway at downtown Dixon and settled into the Holiday Inn. After eating some pizza, we decided to see the sights. I'd never been to Dixon and had no idea this trip was going to take me by it, but if we were there, I decided to make the most of it and learn as much about Reagan as I could. My first memory of him was when, as a 7-year-old, I posted a picture of him cut out of a newspaper on my wall. I really have no way to explain why.

I have a vague recollection of hearing his name talked about in our household as somebody who was going to run for president the following year, 1976. For some reason I decided that he was my kind of guy. I have no memory of him until the following summer when, I clearly recall, my brother and I were clothes shopping and I, transistor radio close to my ear, was listening to live coverage of the Republican National Convention at the exact moment that Reagan lost to President Gerald Ford by 100 delegate votes. I was crushed. I knew very little about politics or history or government; I just knew that my guy had just been defeated.

Back in Dixon, with some time to kill, we went to a gas station and asked for directions to two places I felt I needed to visit to better understand Ronald Reagan: the Rock River where he was said to have saved seventy-seven lives as a lifeguard, and one of his childhood homes on Hennepin Avenue. We drove down a dusty trail to get to the river and spent nearly an hour looking for the famous log that Reagan is said to have carved a notch in for each life he saved. But of course, there was nothing to be found.

So, I decided to call a Reagan biographer named Paul Kengor whom I'd come to know recently, thinking he might know where the elusive log was. A few minutes later Paul was on the line but told me the log is long since gone, swept up into the currents of the feisty Rock River no doubt, lost to history and to strange people like us who care about such things.

A year earlier I had first reached out to Paul with a conversation that went something like this:

"Hello?"

"Hi. May I speak to Paul Kengor please?"

"Speaking."

"Hi. I'm Mark Joseph. You don't know me, but I just wanted to call you and thank you for writing your book on Reagan."

"Oh, sure. You're welcome."

"The reason I wanted to thank you was because it's exactly the book I would have written and thought that I should have written, but was hoping somebody else would so I wouldn't have to, because I'm incredibly lazy. And since you wrote it, it leaves me with one less thing to do in life. So, thanks."

And I meant every word of it. There was something magical about Kengor's work. He had discovered things about Reagan eluding the smartest historians who had tried to decode the mystery that was Ronald Reagan, a man who had famously been declared "inscrutable" by his official biographer. But he wasn't inscrutable to me, nor was he to Kengor, because we understood something about Ronald Reagan that most historians seemed to purposefully misunderstand, namely, the impulses that drove him.

My friend Terry Mattingly, the great syndicated religion columnist, often wrote about what he calls the "ghost" in the stories of people's lives. In his view that ghost is religion, and when the religious impulses that drive us aren't understood, we can often appear to be inscrutable.

On a hunch, Paul had visited the church Reagan grew up attending and asked the current preacher if he could read the sermons Reagan had grown up listening to. The preacher had nodded in the affirmative, then noted that nobody had ever asked to read them, but that Paul would find them in the basement in some boxes.

And that's where Paul found a treasure trove of insights, including evidence that Reagan was not only an attender but an active leader in the church, including teaching Sunday school. With this revelation, the notion perpetuated since at least 1980—that Jimmy Carter was the pious Sunday school teacher while Reagan was a religious phony who skipped church but pretended to be religious to win the votes of the Religious Right—would be put to rest once and for all.

Reagan had in fact traveled back home to Dixon regularly to teach Sunday school at Dixon's Disciples of Christ church during his time away at Eureka College. But more significantly in terms of history, Kengor discovered Reagan's pastor had been something of a staunch anti-Communist who often filled his sermons with rhetoric decrying the Bolshevik Revolution in the Soviet Union. His pastor even invited a Soviet dissident named B.E. Kertchman to visit the church and warn the congregation, including young Ronald Reagan, about the evils of Communism.

Back in modern-day Dixon, after a relaxing afternoon explaining to my kids the significance of the Rock River, visiting the edge of its banks, and playing there as kids are wont to do, we piled into the car. Next stop: the home on Hennepin Avenue and more insights.

The home was white and small, and I stopped in the kitchen and in the upstairs room to think about what the scene looked like seventy-five years earlier when Reagan's mother Nelle busied herself making a meal while her son did his homework. I also stopped to purchase some poems that had been written by Nelle—nothing fancy or even bound, but just a clump of papers that had been stapled together. After taking some pictures in front of the home we were off again, back to the hotel to get ready for my encounter with the judge the next morning.

As I passed through the City Hall metal detectors with my wife and four young daughters in tow the next morning, I quickly found my public defender who told me what I needed to do. I could go to jail, he said, but most likely I'd just have to pay a fine so long as I pleaded guilty. When I explained I was merely traveling at the speed of the car in front of me and that there were cars behind me, he just smiled and said I should tell it to the judge—and in a few short minutes I did just that.

In fact, I also had video footage shot on my cellphone that showed what happened when I tried to go at the speed limit after my citation. Not only were cars honking at me from behind, but one driver sped around my right side and showed me his middle finger. I had the whole thing on tape to prove to the judge that 45 miles an hour was an unreasonable rate of speed.

"How do you plead?" he asked as I stood before him.

"Your honor, I'd like to show you some footage I took to show you what happened when I drove at the speed that was posted," I said with a hopeful tone.

"Son, I'm not going to watch your video," he said. "Now, how do you plead?"

I thought about the public defender's warning about the possibility of jail. And my four young daughters who needed their dad to stay a free man. I quickly replied, "Guilty, Your Honor," and with that I was on my way to the clerk to pay a hefty $500 fine.

The nice lady at the window listened to my story and then looked down at her clipboard. She noted I was the nineteenth case that day, and without exactly saying it, something about her smile left me with the strong impression that this is how Dixon kept their city services funded. *Nineteen people at $500 a head—hey, that would keep a lot of services funded,* I thought.

The fact that I fell prey to this speed trap ultimately didn't matter much because when I got back to California, my Aunt Jeanne, who had heard about my predicament, had sent a check to cover the ticket. And I had come to understand that there was purpose in what had happened and that my trip to Dixon was arranged as part of what Reagan would call the "DP" for me to better understand a man whom I thought I understood.

I can't say that I heard the Voice commanding me to make a movie when I was in Dixon, but I did have a slightly odd moment like the ones in the old *Cold Case* TV series where you get a fleeting glance of somebody from a different era. It wasn't a dream or a vision or anything as concrete as that, just my imagination taking me back in time to a moment when 10-year-old Ronald Reagan was riding his bike home, and I ran into him. In my mind's eye the conversation went something like this:

"Hey. You're Ronald Reagan!"

"Yes sir. Do I know you?"

"You're going to be President of the United States one day."

Looking around, he said, "I don't know who you are or what you're talking about sir. You must have me confused with someone else. I'm just on my way home from baseball practice."

Then, realizing the impossibility of convincing a dirt-poor 10-year-old kid whose father is the town drunk, in the middle of a small town in Illinois, of the role that lies ahead for him, I waved at him and told him I would be on my way. He seemed fine with that and waved back at me. Facing his bike toward home, he rode off.

What I most remember learning from that creative exercise is that American greatness comes from seeming nobodies like young Ronald Reagan in small towns like Dixon, Illinois. I can't speak for the rest of the world, but in America anyway, greatness comes from ordinary places and ordinary people empowered by big ideas and virtues that propel them to accomplish big things—like inventing the airplane, the automobile, and the light bulb and yes, becoming the most powerful person in the world and affecting people's lives around the planet.

We eventually arrived in St. Louis in time for my cousin's wedding. But I went back to California with a renewed sense of purpose. I was going to make a film about Ronald Reagan.

At the time, I was in my fifth year of working for a couple of film companies, Walden Media and Crusader Entertainment, which gave me a front row seat at movies like *The Chronicles of Narnia*, *Ray*, and *Holes*. I worked in the areas of development of the script and marketing on those and other films, as well as producing the soundtrack for *The Passion of The Christ*.

While I enjoyed giving input on a script during the development stage, as well as marketing the film after it was done, handling the part in between, producing the movie, sounded like too much work. But I thought perhaps I needed to rethink my attitude and maybe being in Dixon was part of that process.

Back in Los Angeles, I kept mulling over what had happened back East. A few months later I put in another call to Kengor. Would he give me book rights and allow me to turn Reagan's story into a movie? Paul quickly agreed and the journey of taking Reagan's journey to the big screen began.

2

THE SCREENPLAY

Hiring a writer to write a film screenplay is a lot like getting married. You get to know the person, gather all the information you can about them, but at some point, you go with your gut, follow your heart, and jump. That's how I settled on Jonas McCord as the screenwriter for *Reagan*. Tall, lanky, and appearing to be years younger than his true age, I first met Jonas when I was developing a movie called *Joshua in the City*. Jonas was scheduled to direct, and we talked numerous times about the film, which, as it turned out, was never made.

What I noticed about Jonas was that he carried himself with a confidence bordering on bravado, but he was also humble and personable. A few years back I began to talk to him about my desire to do a movie on Reagan. He seemed lukewarm at the outset and had the annoying habit of calling him "Ronnie" as though they were best friends, but I kept coming back to him as the guy who could write and maybe even direct the picture. As things began to get more serious and when some initial funding came in to develop the screenplay, Jonas and I started to have some serious conversations.

But I was also talking to others. I placed a call to Mike Rich, the award-winning writer of *The Rookie*. He seemed interested but non-committal. I reached out to Randall Wallace, the genius who wrote *Braveheart*, but he was too busy or claimed to be.

I called Joe Eszterhas who wrote *Showgirls* and *Flashdance,* and although he was interested, and I'm sure would have done a great job, it just didn't feel right to me. Finally, the process was winnowed down to two: Jonas and Howie Klausner, a recent friend who had written a Clint Eastwood movie called *Space Cowboys*. I watched *Space Cowboys* and liked Howie's work enough to fly him out to Los Angeles and hear his pitch. It was good.

But when Jonas came in and gave our team his pitch, it was just a little bit better. And when we read examples of Jonas's and Howie's works, we unanimously agreed that Jonas was the choice. I felt the process had been somewhat Reaganesque: although I had a definite feeling that Jonas was the guy, I had listened to my advisors, considered many others, waited to hear the opinions of our team, then made the decision.

We would go with Jonas.

Untold meetings and phone calls later, Jonas and I visited the graves of Nelle and Jack Reagan, Ronald Reagan's parents. I had suggested that we visit the gravesite together as soon as the script was completed. Jonas emailed me the final version of the script just before noon while I was already enroute. Situated on rolling hills in a part of East Los Angeles that may have once upon a time been grand, Nelle and Jack's final resting place looked third world–ish now.

Jonas called to say he was in traffic and running late. Since I had the time, I left the cemetery in search of a flower shop and found flowers for sale on a nearby sidewalk. I picked out a bouquet but learned they didn't take credit cards. I looked in my wallet and saw I only brought $3 with me. I chose a lovely but sparse $3 bouquet.

As I walked the graves, flowers in hand, I saw so many names and dates, some who lived sixty years, a few into their nineties. All were loved, presumably, by someone. Yet that morning, their graves seemed largely unattended and forgotten. And somewhere in the vicinity were the graves of Nelle and Jack. By the time I found them, Jonas was pulling up in his car. He lumbered up the hillside and put an arm on my shoulder as I pointed out the headstones of the two, we had come to visit. We stopped, paused, and stared in silence. After a minute or so we knelt.

I had joked earlier to Jonas that we were going there not to pray to Nelle Reagan, but to God in the presence of her remains. Jonas said a few words, then I began, thanking Him that we had come this far in the process of making the film and asked for guidance. In my prayer I let slip that since Nelle is in heaven, she might also be bugging the Almighty to make our movie a success . . . and to remind God that there is a tradition of mothers pestering Him, as in when a mother of two of the Apostles begged Jesus to allow her sons to sit at Jesus' right and left in heaven.

In a flash we were done. Jonas the Catholic crossed himself. I quietly rose and laid the flowers in between Jack's and Nelle's headstones. I know that beneath them are merely bones, but I also knew the ground we were standing on was the ground their son likely visited after they had passed.

Someone once said that women rule the world through their children. I think of how Nelle Reagan effectively ruled the world from a grave, tucked away in the inner city of Los Angeles. I'm reminded again how powerful women have always been, even when we or they don't realize it.

While we had reached an important milestone in our film, we had major hills yet to climb. But we'd planted our flag. And now we begin the process of taking the screenplay and beating it into submission. That process turned out to be more than I bargained for. For me, a Reagan screenplay was like pizza: I even like the not so good ones, which is why Little Caesar's has done brisk business all these years.

I decided to send the screenplay out to a few trusted friends and colleagues. Rachelle, a former intern, loved to read scripts and promised to come out of retirement for a Target gift card. The president of a studio I'd been talking to agreed to read. My mentor and producer of *X-Men*, Ralph Winter, agreed to read as did my friend and colleague John Sullivan, and another mentor, Howard Kazanjian, no slouch of a producer himself having produced *Return of the Jedi* and *Raiders of the Lost Ark*.

The trouble started almost immediately, and I was buffeted from all directions: The head of the studio said it was unusable. Howard and Ralph weighed in with similarly negative comments as did John, and now my world was turned upside down. Did I make the wrong call here? Should I have gone with someone else? I'm sure Reagan faced these kinds of questions as well. Surely, he felt this way after the Marine barracks were blown up or maybe when he decided to go to Bitburg, the Nazi cemetery that Jewish leaders begged him not to visit. But I didn't think I had. I thought Jonas was still our man, but we needed major work, and he was not likely to be happy.

Now I realized that in my zeal to make sure that Reagan's childhood wasn't lost in a story about his presidency, I'd caused Jonas to go down a path that was too focused on his childhood. At my urging, he had traveled to Dixon and on to Reagan's alma mater, Eureka College. At each stop along the way he would call excitedly upon making new acquaintances and gaining new understandings about Reagan the boy and young man. But now our film had become a childhood drama at the expense of Reagan the President.

I called for a meeting with some of my friends who were interested in helping me review the script–Jonas, Ralph, and John–and we settled into my friend Phil's offices in Burbank for a two-hour script meeting. I praised Jonas for his work and then expressed my feeling that we needed a lot more of President Reagan.

Ralph said he had read through the script once but needed to read over the material again to confirm his feeling there were structural problems to be addressed. John gave an impassioned plea for the need to scale back the early years while adding in more about Reagan's Hollywood years and his first meeting with Nancy. Through this process I learned more about Jonas: He was open to new ideas, once he got past the initial shock and defensiveness. And perhaps this is something I've always sensed about him: He feels things strongly but is always open to new ideas, provided he has a chance to digest them and make them his own.

That didn't mean we didn't have fireworks. One night as I drove up the 101, I found myself screaming at Jonas's resistance to including more of Reagan as President.

"You have to remember that during the time Reagan was serving as President, you hated him, so you have no strong memories of what he did, but our audience does," I yelled.

"We can't do everything in a two-hour movie," he screamed back. "That's a different movie you're talking about."

"No, it's not," I countered. "His fans have certain expectations. They don't want to hear page after page of dialogue between Reagan's childhood girlfriend's parents, at the expense of seeing him win the election in 1980. And we're not going to be taken seriously if we don't cover Iran-Contra."

Jonas argued back and we called a truce; he agreed to give it some more thought.

3

ONE CHANCE TO MAKE A FIRST IMPRESSION

I optioned Kengor's book rights in January of 2006 and hoped every day since that nobody else would come up with the bright idea to make a Reagan movie. I knew of a Ridley Scott movie that focused on Reagan and Gorbachev's weekend in Reykjavik, but that didn't trouble me too much since I couldn't imagine that normal people would care much for a movie like that.

I once talked to an employee at a major studio who had a notion to make a movie on Reagan, and I heard some rumblings that another Reagan movie was being made by a producer friend. But nothing much seemed to come of them. Still, in Hollywood, once a movie is announced about a particular person or topic, it's very hard to follow in its wake. If one of them were to announce, it would mean trouble for us, so I monitored them carefully.

One day I discovered an article from an obscure Midwestern newspaper about a man who was boasting that movie rights to his book on Reagan had been acquired by a small production company. The more I read, the stranger the film became as it had less to do with Reagan and more to do with a character who engaged in some sort of time travel and happened to travel back in time to when Reagan was a lifeguard.

No major threat to us, but a danger nonetheless and as ridiculous as the premise sounded, major media would likely pick up on any movie being made about Reagan and crown it as "The One." I knew our days of toiling in obscurity must end. After conferring with the others, I began developing a plan to release the information about our movie in a major way.

My friend Paul, a veteran journalist with the *Hollywood Reporter,* was the only member of the media that I had trusted with the story. He often reminded me that when I was ready for the story to come out, he wanted to be the one to write it. I told Paul it was time, and he interviewed me and several of the others associated with the film.

The story was set to run.

Two days before publication date, I was still a little concerned: Did he get any facts wrong? Had I explained anything incorrectly? I asked Paul to meet for breakfast. Although I rarely eat sweet breakfasts, this morning I ordered a big waffle with strawberries and whipped cream, and we began our debrief.

"I can only lose my movie virginity on this story one time, so I just want to make sure it's accurate," I told Paul. He asked me more questions and when it seemed as if there were no misunderstandings and he'd gotten the story right, we moved on to other topics and enjoyed the remaining moments of our breakfast.

As we walked out of the diner and headed toward our cars, I was confident that Paul would get the story right. I wasn't disappointed. Two days later he texted me excitedly, noting that his editors were going to hold the story until the following day because of the impact they believed it was going to have.

Believing that the story wouldn't be hitting until the following morning, I went to dinner with my wife, kids, and parents-in-law to celebrate their wedding anniversary. I made it through most of a leisurely dinner at a fondue restaurant without checking my email. But at the end of the evening, I casually sneaked a peek at my iPhone and discovered that the news had broken a day early.

The story was so hot its release was being sped up, the reporter would later tell me. I read through the story breathlessly, hoping there was nothing incorrect that might create problems. To my relief Paul got everything correct.

There *was* one small thing I realized could quickly mushroom into a large misunderstanding: Paul quoted Jonas as saying that he had thought Reagan was a buffoon and a bad actor, leaving the impression that he still thought that way.

Immediately conservative bloggers registered their objections, fearing that Reagan's story was now in the hands of a man who thinks he's an idiot. Realizing the importance of putting out this fire quickly, within forty-eight hours I gave two interviews making it clear that Jonas was merely saying how he had once felt before delving into the character. But in the meantime, I had waited to see if the story about my little movie would be picked up by the all-important Drudge Report.

I have always understood the power of Matt Drudge. I first met Matt in the late 1990s when he was living in Hollywood, driving a red hatchback and had just launched his fledgling website. When a mutual friend would guest on *Politically Incorrect*, we would sometimes go to dinner together along with the show's host, Bill Maher. I always enjoyed his company. He was witty, smart, loquacious, and very conservative.

I was hoping *The Hollywood Reporter*'s story on my film would also catch Drudge's attention, but trying to plan such an event was like trying to catch the wind. Drudge is not unlike the Soup Nazi, that infamous Seinfeld character who is nearly impossible to predict, but whose favor one must at least try to curry, nonetheless.

By the next morning Drudge had indeed conferred his

magic link, and our movie was now front and center and in the media bloodstream. I was elated. Taking a screen shot of the magic moment, I cheered inside. *Reagan: The Movie* was now officially a big deal.

In the days ahead our little announcement was picked up by hundreds of outlets like *The Washington Post, Fox News, CNN,* and *MTV*, as well as dozens of foreign media. I knew there would be many battles ahead, yet I breathed a sigh of relief as I savored the fact that we had made the most out of our one and only moment to make a first impression with our movie.

4

THE DISTRICT

I'm ashamed to admit the last time I had been in Washington, D.C. I was twenty years younger. All I can say is that the intervening two decades were busy ones, I had no real business there, and that for many years I disliked flying and travel enough to avoid going places I didn't have to. Plus, I could get all my D.C. from watching my favorite show, *Hardball with Chris Matthews*, and reading various political columnists. So why actually go there?

When the film was announced, I knew I needed to go and visit with those who knew Reagan well, and to secure funding, which is how my daughter Anna and I found ourselves in Washington, D.C., or "The District" as I quickly learned to call it.

One of our earliest cheerleaders offered to host a dinner for us and gathered a couple of dozen of his friends, and we had a delightful evening talking about the movie. Later at another dinner, I found myself at a table with a middle-aged gentleman who told me just how big our film was going to be, then recounted an incredible story about how, after Reagan died, he flew from South Dakota to California to try to get into the line of people who were allowed to pass by Reagan's closed coffin at the Reagan Library and Museum.

By the time he got close to the library he was told they would not take any more people. He went back to his son's apartment crestfallen, only to come up with Plan B: He would fly to Washington, D.C. and position himself on a sidewalk where the vehicle carrying Reagan would pass by. And that's exactly what this grown man did—acting like a 16-year-old Beatles fan might have in 1964. Such is the power that Ronald Reagan had over average Americans.

My first meeting with those who knew Reagan was with Frank Fahrenkopf, former chairman of the Republican National Committee. Frank told me this story: Once he and Reagan landed around midnight in Las Vegas and were being driven from the airport when Frank noticed some of Las Vegas's finest women were waving at the President seated next to him in the limousine. Several lifted their tops off in a risqué salute. For years, Frank said, Reagan would, at various seemingly serious presidential moments, lean over and joke with Frank of that most unusual Vegas welcome.

Others have more serious stories to tell.

Gary Bauer, former domestic policy advisor to Reagan, told me how various non-conservatives in the White House tried to sabotage his attempts to bring certain issues to the President's attention and how, despite that, Bauer continued to do so. Reagan eventually grew to understand what was happening and made sure that Bauer was allowed to speak freely without being muzzled by more senior officials.

In meeting after meeting, I explained our predicament: I needed to raise $30 million to produce the film and another $20 million to market and distribute it. Many people I met said they were confident the film would get funded. But nobody wrote a check. It may be obvious, but I quickly learn that conservatives are conservative with their money and liberals are liberal with their cash.

I attended two meetings of conservatives, one where the median age was about 35 and another where it was about 60. At both I had three minutes to speak, and I told them about my little movie and asked for their support. Later, at the younger of the two meetings a man gave me his card and said he wanted to help, and he knew tons of billionaires.

I'd heard that before.

Anna and I decided to do some sightseeing, and we posed for the obligatory pictures in front of the White House, the U.S. Capitol, and the Washington Hilton, or as it's called these days apparently, The Hinckley Hilton. As we pulled up to the Hilton, I recognize it instantly as the place where Reagan nearly died, and I wondered how different the world would have been if that bullet had moved a third of an inch and lodged in his heart.

I got out of the car and looked closely at the rounded brownish wall that was just as it was in pictures I'd seen hundreds of times. I remember the day as though it were yesterday. I was fast asleep when my mother burst into my room and turned on my radio in time for me to hear the coverage of Reagan being shot.

He had escaped the fate that had struck down another hero from another time, John F. Kennedy. I think it's a perfectly plausible scenario to think that the '60s might not have happened as they did, had JFK not been gunned down as he had.

Nobody can say what would or wouldn't have happened in Vietnam, but I'm sure that for millions of American young people, watching their young president be gunned down in such a tragic way in some sense contributed to the restless and the angst that so symbolized the counterculture. Who knows what Reagan's untimely demise, just two months after becoming president, might have produced in my culture? I can't say and I'm certainly glad that I didn't have to find out.

We were careful to maintain that sense of wonder on

Reagan's part at having had his life spared, as we worked through the script. Shortly after returning to the White House, he was said to have asked his aides to send a religious leader over, and the aides decided to send Cardinal Cooke, who spoke with Reagan and heard the leader of the free world say that he believed that God had spared his life and that whatever time he had left was dedicated to serving Him.

He even indicated to one interviewer that perhaps the shooting had been allowed by God to humble him a bit. Reagan confessed maybe he'd gotten a bit prideful, understandable considering the landslide election he'd just won over President Carter.

As I thought of how to portray these emotions in our movie, I remembered a line I'd read from Alexander Haig's book *Caveat*, which I had read at the tender age of 14—weird, I know. Haig, a military man before becoming Reagan's first Secretary of State, recounted the story of the Roman generals who were said to have, upon returning from conquering a foreign land, been lauded with an open chariot parade, but also provided with an aide whose job was to crouch in the chariot and recite for the General's benefit, "Remember, you are human."

It was perfectly plausible that Haig might have shared that story with Reagan and it fit what I imagined might have been going through Reagan's mind: Providence had been in full control that day, working through the twisted mind of John Hinckley to accomplish His purpose in Reagan's life; to remind him that he was human, and that the moment of his death would be determined by God alone and that Reagan was to serve humbly and not think too highly of himself.

Reagan later said as he lay at the hospital staring death in the face, he had the clear feeling that he wouldn't recover unless he forgave Hinckley for what he had done. It's also interesting to think about how his God eventually allowed his life to slip away by taking from him the thing that drove the Reagan

Revolution—his mind and imagination—as though reminding him and us once again that he was still, after all, merely a man.

It all reminds me of the King of Babylon, Nebuchadnezzar, who lost his mind when he failed to worship God, and was reduced to eating grass like an animal, only to have God later restore him to his throne. Reagan had been spared and reminded, perhaps–if he needed reminding as we all do from time to time–that he was just a man.

As I wrapped up our time in D.C., at lunch at the next table I saw a disgraced former member of Congress who was forced to resign when his extramarital affairs were revealed. As I headed to the airport our cab driver told me, "Many great men are brought down by sex." I wonder how Reagan managed to avoid that fatal mistake that has taken down so many politicians.

As our plane prepared to take off, I reflected on the people I had met and the many stories about the man from Dixon that seem to pour out of people in the city he called home for eight years. The journey to understand Reagan to make this movie was just beginning, but as I met with those who knew him best, I was starting to understand him better.

5

STANFORD

Back in California, I was invited to Stanford University in Palo Alto to meet with Ed Meese, perhaps Reagan's most trusted aide and loyal friend. Everybody spoke highly of Meese. He seemed to have few enemies. So, I got in the car and drove six hours to meet with him only to be told by him that after our meeting was over, he would be getting on a plane to Los Angeles from where I had just traveled.

Oh well. Still, finding that out in our meeting didn't dampen my enthusiasm for gleaning insights about Reagan from a man who worked closely with him for two plus decades.

Meese had a slight limp. As I followed him around the Stanford campus to his office and then to a café, I looked around and saw students passing by him without taking notice of him. For years I carefully studied the cast of characters around Reagan, and Meese was the one who seemed the most honest, loyal, trustworthy, and gracious.

There were rogues of course, Alexander Haig with his massive ego for instance. But Meese just seemed to ooze loyalty, and Reagan returned the favor by refusing to fire him or distance himself from him when he was dogged by ethics charges.

I had an hour with Meese and used every minute. I carefully studied his face, eyes, and hair. He really hadn't changed much in thirty years; perhaps he gained a few pounds and added a bit of silver to his hair. Other than that, he was just as I imagined him—jolly-looking, self-deprecating, humble, gracious, and never prone to exaggerating anything in any way.

At one point I asked him if he wasn't the closest thing Reagan had to a kid brother. Meese thought about it for a moment and then nodded in agreement. He quickly added that even so, there were certain areas beyond which he couldn't go, areas reserved for Nancy, and perhaps even areas reserved for no other human being. Meese mentioned he and Reagan once talked about their kids, but otherwise it seemed to me that the relationship was always cordial and, although as close as anybody could be with Reagan, still slightly distant.

Later he told me he never visited the inner sanctum of Reagan's ranch house. Only after Reagan died did Meese visit the house and saw that Reagan had proudly displayed a painting Meese had given him. Before long, our sandwiches were eaten and our time was gone, but two more meetings ensued at Stanford: one with former Secretary of State George Shultz that included former economic advisor Marty Anderson and his wife, Annelise, and the other with former speechwriter Peter Robinson.

I met with Robinson outdoors on the campus and he shared stories of his time as speechwriter. I was surprised to learn he was one of the architects of the Brandenburg gate speech. He was both outgoing and modest about his work with Reagan, a trait I don't often find.

The Andersons were ready for our meeting. They presented me with a dozen or so briefing books containing declassified materials from National Security meetings that would prove to be invaluable. To hear how administration officials spoke to

each other in meetings helped our team gain a keen understanding of what was going on behind the scenes.

We sat down for a meeting in their conference room, and it
quickly became apparent that Marty had an agenda—to
convince me that Reagan wasn't very religious at all. He handed
me an article from a fan magazine from 1950 in which Reagan
appeared to downplay his faith.

Even though I knew what he was up to, I was nonetheless
grateful to have even one bit of counterbalancing information
to everything else I'd heard and read contradicting this. That's
how I had to approach Reagan as a storyteller—to let the
evidence take me where it wants to go.

I quizzed them both about why they weren't in the administration and from what I gathered, Marty was pushed aside by
other aides jockeying for position, and he didn't have the
stomach for such games. Still, I got the sense Marty played a
powerful role in the months leading up to Reagan's election
while Annelise had done important work after Reagan's presidency in gathering information for several books on his time in
office.

My first meeting with George Shultz happened in his office
at Stanford. He was 90 or so but in amazing shape mentally and
physically. Sitting across from him I was struck by his piercing
eyes and quickly realized this is what the Soviets must have
faced in negotiations. He seemed to look right through me, as
though he was analyzing and studying my face and every word
that came out of my mouth.

For all I knew, he was planning to leave the meeting and get
right on the phone with Nancy Reagan, so I was mindful to
choose my words carefully. He gave us important information
that first day, but I'd be back several times to visit with him to
get his character right. As we parted, he gave me a copy of his
autobiography, which proved to be a very useful source of
information, particularly because it's within those pages I

learned that Shultz has a tattoo of a tiger on his rear end, a homage to his alma mater's mascot.

I'd use that tidbit in the film later when his Soviet counterpart called him "the tiger man," which resulted in one of my favorite lines from the film. In the scene, Jon Voight's character "Viktor" responded to a query from his young Russian counterpart as to how he knew this: "KGB!" Viktor replied.

6

HAPPY BIRTHDAY MR. PRESIDENT

Had Ronald Reagan been alive in 2011, he would have been turning 100. The nation celebrated the milestone of his birth. There were moments when I regretted our movie wasn't ready to release in theaters, but I came back to the knowledge of the DP, that He knew the best moment for the film to be released, and was engineering those circumstances even through what I thought were failures on my part that caused delays.

It is what it is: the nation turned to celebrate Ronald Reagan, and my movie hadn't even started production yet. So, I began a four-day weekend of attending various Reagan events to meet more people who knew him. On the first night I was in Newport Beach at an event hosted by a think tank where the originator of what came to be known as "Reaganomics," Arthur Laffer, was speaking. It was while talking with him that I came upon another clue in my quest to understand Reagan: Laffer told me Reagan was only interested in discussing economics.

Yet when I talked to the more religiously minded, they told me he only wanted to discuss biblical prophecies. I came to the realization that Reagan intuited what you were interested in and focused on that, and didn't delve much into topics he knew didn't interest you. Consequently, each person in each camp believed he was only interested in the things they were interested into the exclusion of the other topics.

It sort of reminds me of the blind men who came face-to-face with an elephant. Each had hands on a different part of the animal, and each thought the animal was a trunk or a leg or tail or whatever—and they were all partially right, but not totally.

Laffer famously came up with what came to be known as the "Laffer Curve"—the notion that once taxation exceeded a certain amount it caused less revenue to be collected. Laffer regaled the audience with remembrances of Reagan. Over the next decade I spent lots of time with Art in person and on the phone. I called him whenever I was stumped by something.

I quickly figured out from talking to him that Reagan came to believe in what would be called Reaganomics largely because of Art, who was in his late twenties when he and Reagan began having lunches together. Art was a favorite of one of Reagan's kitchen cabinet members, Justin Dart, and no doubt Reagan took him seriously because of the Dart connection.

Art told me that over those lunches, he laid out for Reagan the merits of tax cutting as a means of spurring economic growth, and Reagan became convinced. I'm not sure whether Reagan learned about it from Art or from his economics classes at Eureka College, but I used a line in the film that Reagan sometimes shared—about Ibn Khaldun, an Egyptian ruler, who ruled in the 12th century and who found the connection between cutting taxes and more revenue to the government.

Art was an optimist and was always encouraging during the process of putting the film together. Later, after we announced Dennis Quaid as our choice to play Reagan, I introduced him to Dennis at dinner one night where all three of us were set to speak at a meeting of the Friends of Ronald Reagan, and we all got along famously.

Art also gave me one of the most valuable and interesting insights into Reagan the man: He told me that the moment he first set eyes on Reagan he knew he was the son of an alcoholic because Reagan always strived for physical perfection—never a hair out of place and always dressed impeccably. All things children of alcoholic fathers do so as not to trigger Dad's anger, Art observed.

Reagan's centennial celebrations continued, and this time the party resumed at Reagan's beloved ranch, Rancho del Cielo, which is translated "Ranch in the heavens." The ranch was purchased by a group known as the Young Americans Foundation, which promptly restored it and built a center nearby in which they hosted events for Reagan aficionados.

It was my second visit to the ranch, and I was there with the reporter John Fund. We walked a trail from the ranch house up a slight hill and headed toward the stable where Reagan kept his horses. As we walked, John told me he spent time with Reagan in high school when the then-governor began holding sessions with high school students called "Meet the Governor," during which Reagan took questions from them.

"Why high-schoolers and not college students?" I asked John.

"Because he said it was often too late to reach them by the time they were in college," he said with a laugh. "You had to catch them while they were in high school before they were indoctrinated by their college professors."

I learned that John was a Lutheran and a bachelor, and that his views were shaped and molded by Reagan, whose ideas lived on through John's work as a columnist. We continued walking, this time up to the trailer-type facility that had served as the Secret Service agents' quarters. As we walked in, John, the ever-curious reporter, began to page through the agent logs from yesteryear, and in a flash, one of the docents asked him not to do so because the material was classified.

We both got a laugh out of that one but listened carefully

when another official told us how Reagan, ever the gracious host, upon learning that Nancy was gone for the evening, called up and asked if the agents would mind if he stopped by with popcorn and a movie to watch with them. I have a feeling they didn't mind at all.

Back at the ranch house, I breezed past former ABC newsman Sam Donaldson, who happened to be in town this day and wanted to see the house where the man that he seemed to relish interrogating had lived. He'd been there before, of course, shouting questions at then President Reagan, but perhaps he wanted to come back one last time to pay his respects. I wondered what he thought, but never stopped to ask.

Leaving the ranch behind, I headed back to the Center where a panel discussion was taking place, a discussion including one of Reagan's fiercest critics, Lou Cannon. Cannon had covered Reagan as a reporter beginning in his gubernatorial days but on this day was oddly respectful of the man that he had, in the past, often written critically of. I couldn't tell what had prompted his seeming change-of-heart about Reagan, but something had changed.

The final event was a dinner followed by a speech by Sarah Palin. As I watched her, I thought, *She's no Ronald Reagan.* Then again, maybe Ronald Reagan wasn't always Ronald Reagan. After all, for Palin, in Reagan years, it was still 1957 or so, still two decades away from his rendezvous with destiny.

Contrasting the two leaders, Palin spoke in generalities, Reagan in concrete terms, often salted with stories to help illustrate his point. I wondered what Reagan would think of Palin, without a doubt an ideological heir of his—one who just hadn't put in the time Reagan had, devouring newspapers, magazines, and books, and listening carefully to the many smart people he seemed to often have around him.

The next day I was off to the Reagan Library for a two-day celebration. I arrived and mingled among former Reagan staffers, friends, and who knows whom else, another chance to try to understand the man by talking to those who knew him best. I saw a man with a full head of dark hair sitting alone at a table reading Kengor's book *God & Ronald Reagan*.

When I asked him about it, we chatted, and he introduced himself as Emilio Garza. I instantly recognized him as a judge whom Reagan had nominated for a judgeship and who had almost been nominated for the seat that later went to Clarence Thomas. As we chatted for a bit, I marveled that Garza traveled from Texas to be at this celebration. People loved Reagan. Even in death. I am constantly amazed by this.

The next day it was time for the official party. Hundreds of us gathered on a lawn outside of the library to be entertained by the Beach Boys, Amy Grant, Michael W. Smith, and others. Having spent a lot of time with Reagan's closest pals, I was amazed that none of them were featured at the event. Instead, the honor of being asked to give the main speech went to James Baker who, came to the Reagan administration through his friend George H.W. Bush.

Later Mrs. Reagan walked haltingly to her husband's gravesite and laid a wreath accompanied by Baker. Another concert featured the Beach Boys and during the grand finale luncheon I found myself seated next to two children of Mike Love of the Beach Boys.

On Super Bowl Sunday there was one last party to attend and, amazingly, it included one of the most meaningful encounters of the weekend. During a party at Congressman Elton Gallegly's house, I sat next to an elderly couple who were parked in front of a big-screen TV and introduced myself. To my surprise the man's wife introduced herself and then her husband, Peter Hannaford. Wow. *He has lost a lot of hair*, I thought. *And he's aged quite a bit.* He looked quite different from the man on the back of the dust jacket of his book I had at home.

We hit it off instantly and when I told him what I was doing he became excited. After some conversation, I leaned in and asked him to tell me some things about Reagan I may have missed. Movies about perfect people are boring and I needed to find the dark side . . . if there was one.

"Would he ever get angry?" I asked.

Hannaford proceeded to tell me that, yes, he did get angry occasionally, recounting a time when his staff had over-scheduled him and Reagan, upon seeing the schedule, Reagan threw his glasses across the conference table and demanded a lighter schedule. I jocularly asked him if he had any dirt on Reagan, because everybody I talked to only seemed to have good things to say about him. Hannaford grinned a bit and made me promise that I wouldn't use it in the film.

"Promise," I replied, and he launched into a story about a time when Reagan came into a meeting and announced that he was going to instigate a psychological warfare campaign against the Soviets. Excited aides quickly asked him for more information, and he said the campaign would involve the creation of giant condoms.

Perplexed, the aides dutifully wrote down Reagan's words only to have him add, "I want you to inscribe on them: Made in the USA: Size small."

Hannaford quickly reminded me that such jokes were only uttered by Reagan among men, never in the presence of women. Chivalry, I guess. The afternoon was soon over. On the long drive home from Simi Valley, I was left with my thoughts and the remembrances of others who loved this man. Slowly, one person at a time, I was discovering the man, warts and all, that would grow into a character who would make for what I hoped will be a compelling film.

7

THE SCREENPLAY PART 2

The second draft of the screenplay arrived on my iPhone, and I began to read. I shouldn't have been doing so but I did. I was scheduled to leave for Chicago on a 4 p.m. flight, leaving four children and an exhausted wife behind, so I decided I needed to spend a little quality time with the family. We were at a restaurant called Millie's waiting for our order to arrive when I absentmindedly checked my messages and saw that Howie had just sent in forty-eight pages of the screenplay.

I couldn't resist peeking before I had a chance to go home and print it to read on the airplane. As I quickly glanced through the script, I teared up. Nothing unusual there, as I'd teared up reading various versions along the way. I suppose it's better than not tearing up. Anyway, after a few minutes I set it aside and resumed being dad and husband and look forward to reading it on the plane. At home the printer was jammed so I dashed off to the office to print it and later, on the plane, read through Howie's first stab.

He's nailed it, I thought.

Before choosing Jonas to write the first draft, I had polled each of the members of my team. It was close, but the consensus was Jonas by a whisker. Although it was ultimately my call, I listened carefully to each member and pulled the trigger, picking Jonas. But after some mixed reviews of Jonas's script, I knew what had to be done.

At a small coffee shop in West Los Angeles, I ordered chicken noodle soup and waited for Jonas to arrive. When he did, he ordered a coffee, and I proceeded to break the news. "I need a fresh set of eyes on Reagan," I said, or something like that, telling him that he had taken the project as far as he could and I needed him to hand the baton to another writer, Howie. I had no idea what to expect.

Would he explode and tell me off?

I wasn't used to hiring and firing writers and waited for the explosion. It never came. Jonas was a class act.

"I've been rewritten by the best of them—by Aaron Sorkin," he said. "I get it." If he was disappointed, he hid it well. I made it clear he was still a candidate to direct, and although he seemed doubtful about that, we moved on to the start-up he was launching. Half an hour later we parted ways and the conversation that had been weighing so heavily on my mind was behind me.

Howie clearly relished the opportunity to take a second bite of the apple. "I had a feeling this was going to happen," he said in his typically cheerful voice. Always looking at the glass as half-full, that's Howie—a lot like Reagan himself, I thought. Whereas Jonas was somber, introspective, serious, and somewhat complicated, Howie was joyful, excitable, and always ready with a quick laugh.

He was going to be in California for the holidays with his wife's family and we would have plenty of time to work together. It would be a page-one rewrite, industry speak for basically completely starting over again.

One of the lines that Reagan's mother says in the film, "Remember Whose you are and Whom you serve," was something straight out of my childhood said to me by my mother a thousand times as I headed for the door to go to school. We kept that. Otherwise, it was Howie's turn, and he was confident that he had what he needed and began working, occasionally checking in with me to know how he was progressing.

Writers are all very different, of course, and when John had first mentioned to Jonas that we needed a treatment he shrugged it off by saying he didn't do treatments, a sort of synopsis that often precedes a full-blown screenplay. Howie, on the other hand, felt as though he needed to start with a treatment which he would then share with us, and which would allow us to see where he was headed.

Then, later, he would add the dialogue, and we'd have our screenplay. The process went almost exactly as advertised, although he ended up turning it in in April instead of March, which he had been shooting for. But soon we would both be in for a surprise that would turn the entire process upside down.

8

THE DREAM

I joke that God only speaks to me in dreams when I'm not listening to Him in the daytime, and it wasn't lost on me that I share a name with the most famous dreamer in the Bible. But mostly I either don't dream or don't remember them, and for that I'm sort of grateful, especially when I hear of the horrible nightmares people have.

I must not have been listening to the Man Upstairs on January 12th, because that night I woke up with a doozy. I wouldn't even call it a dream—more like the state I'm in when I'm starting to awake. I've learned to recognize when something important has been placed in my brain and that if I don't write it down as soon as I awake, I may fall back asleep and be unable to remember it in the morning.

On this morning, I was clearly seeing how the movie was supposed to open, in my half awake, half dreaming state of mind. I saw everything very clearly and in vivid detail. A 90-ish KGB agent in an old folks' home in Russia was looking at me, speaking clearly and crisply, so clearly and crisply that I later wrote down these words:

Shot of man in nursing home in Russia or on the porch of a country dacha looking out over a parched land. In a thick Russian accent, he speaks:

"My name is Viktor Petrovich Ivanov and I am the man responsible for the fall of the Soviet Union. I was a lowly young KGB agent in 1946 assigned to cover a young actor named Ronald Reagan who was causing problems for us in Hollywood. My mission was to protect the motherland from all enemies, foreign and domestic, and I realized right away that Reagan was a deadly enemy to the nation that I loved.

"I was alone in that realization, however, because I could never get my comrades to take him seriously. Until it was too late. My warnings were dismissed because he was just an actor, a man whose ideas were so out of fashion that he could never be elected to any position that would threaten our nation. But I never dismissed him. For years my dossier on Ronald Reagan grew—I gathered every bit of information I could on the man because I feared for the motherland.

"But nobody would listen to a lowly KGB agent warning about the man who promised to lead a crusade against the nation we cherished. And nobody but I feared the Crusader until it was too late. This is his story."

Next, I clearly saw Petrovich walking down a long marble-floored hallway with rounded, high, white ceilings. He was holding a dossier that had an 8" x 10" photo of young Reagan on the outside of it. He was on his way into the heart of the Kremlin to deliver the news to an incredulous General Secretary Brezhnev that Ronald Reagan was about to be elected President of the United States.

I woke myself up, grabbed my computer, and wrote a note to Howie telling him that the last thing I wanted to do was to tell my writer how to write a script, but that I wanted to pass on to him an interesting thing that had come to me in the night. With some trepidation, I sent my note to him, but didn't tell him where my idea was from. I didn't want to micro-manage his creative process beyond what was necessary. I waited for his response, which came shortly thereafter:

> That's great! Been working on this, this is the best flow and structure so far. I'll put together an outline/beat sheet for you. Once you're happy with it, I'm off to the races.

It was perfect, he said, and proceeded to tell me that he had been searching for a device that could both open the picture and provide the way to tell the story to the audience. For Howie, Viktor not only provided the opening he needed, but would be the vantage point from which Reagan's story would be told, and it would be a nearly all-knowing one at that since, next to God Himself, only a KGB agent would likely have known as much about Reagan.

Voilà, just like that, we had our narrator for the film.

It was exhilarating to realize I had been the conduit for such an important part of our movie. I'd produced movies before, but this one was different, and I guarded my preroga-tives zealously, making sure I was able to guide the project creatively. I had watched up close as Mel Gibson kept all creative and marketing decisions close to the vest. As a result, Mel was able to turn on a dime and make quick decisions that would have taken months in an entrenched bureaucracy that most studios are.

I also watched my beloved Narnia movies succumb to bureaucratic bumbling and a misguided director who seemed determined to undermine the message of the movies. Now, I was equally determined to avoid these things. I never imagined delivering to my writer the film's opening and the device by which the story was to be told. But that's the way things were unfolding. Still, unsure as to whether Howie was just humoring me, I tried my new opening out on different people and, without exception, everybody loved it.

It was to be a few years before I would have another revelation that would help develop the character of Viktor further. I began to do a deep dive on Soviet-era spies and how they monitored Americans who they might perceive to be a threat to their country.

Of course, we all know about honeypots, attractive women who would be set up to snag the affections of their targets. I had no doubt this strategy was employed against Reagan, as it was likely to have been employed against others who had been outspoken against the Soviet Union.

Spending time in the bowels of the Reagan Library, I pored over documents and focused on the Stasi Files, intelligence gathered about Americans compiled by the Communist East Germans and shared with their Soviet counterparts. Reagan was deemed to be superstitious and a teetotaler, and several of his associates who were most threatening, including Antonin Scalia and Gary Bauer, were specifically mentioned.

Another particularly interesting series of documents were the FBI files on Reagan, which often consisted of interviews with friends, associates, and even neighbors. I found a common theme in many of them that went something like this: "He's a very nice guy, but very extreme in his views."

My most fascinating find was discovering a historical figure who would help me flesh out Viktor. Although I couldn't find any records of Soviet agents who had tracked Reagan a la Viktor, I did come across a tantalizing figure who would give me clues as to how Viktor might have thought.

His name was Yuri Bezmenov, a real-life Soviet spy who defected to the West. Bezmenov had published several works after defecting, but I was most taken by a lecture he gave in which he advised the West how to beat the Soviet Union.

I was particularly fascinated by his notion that it was faith, not force, that would be the key to bringing down the Evil Empire. He said:

"Civilizations like Mohenjo-daro in the River Indus area, like Egypt, like Maya, Incas, like Babylonian culture collapsed and disappeared from the surface of Earth the moment they lost religion. As simple as that. They disintegrated. Nobody remembers about them anymore."

Bezmenov continued his address to an American audience:

"All this sophisticated technology and computers will not prevent society from disintegrating and eventually dying out." Taking chalk to a chalkboard in a classroom setting, he wrote out "2 x 2 = 4" then said, "Have you ever met a person who would sacrifice his life, freedom, for the truth like that? This is truth. I have never met a person who said, 'This is truth and I'm ready, shoot me' to defend the truth,' right?"

He continued:

"But millions sacrifice their life, freedom, comfort, everything for things like God, like Jesus Christ. It's an honor. Some martyrs in the Soviet concentration camps died, and they died in peace, unlike those who shouted 'Long live Stalin!' knowing perfectly well that you may not live long. Something which is not material, moves society and helps it to survive and the other way around, the moment we turn into 'two by two is four' and make it a guiding principle of our life, our existence, we die."

Bezmenov went on to say:

"Even though this is true, and this we cannot prove, you only can feel and have faith in it. So, the answer to ideological

subversion strangely enough is very simple. You don't have to
shoot people. You don't have to aim missiles and Pershing's
and cruise missiles . . . You simply must have faith and prevent
subversion. In other words, to not be a victim of subversion
don't try to be a person who in judo is trying to smash your
enemy and being caught by your hand. Don't strike like that.
Strike with the power of your spirit and moral superiority. If
you don't have that power, it's high time to develop it. And
that's the only answer. That's it."

I was stunned and amazed, for Bezmenov helped to flesh
out Viktor. What I especially appreciated was the fact that
though he was making a spiritual or religious argument, it
didn't appear to come from a place of his own faith but rather a
kind of objective analysis of what moves people and civilizations.

Regarding how Viktor "came" to me, of course there may be
some who would understandably explain my good fortune by
saying that getting the script right was weighing heavily on my
mind as I went to bed the night before, and that my subcon-
scious was working through the issues as I slept, spitting out
the answer the next morning as I drifted toward consciousness.
Others will see the hand of Providence guiding. Whichever you
believe, it's all still part of the magic of creating something
special for the big screen.

As I sat on an airplane headed to Chicago I read Howie's
brilliant work, weaving a tale of the early life of Ronald Reagan
as told through the eyes and words of a KGB agent whose only
goal was to protect the only way of life he'd ever known from a
man who sought its destruction.

Howie was determined to turn in the script by midnight
but, knowing I had some time on the plane, he agreed to send
me the first forty-eight pages, which took me from Viktor
through Reagan's childhood and on to the moment when
Reagan left for Hollywood and saw his dreams of marrying his

childhood love, Margaret "Mugs" Cleaver, go up in smoke when she broke up with him and headed to Paris.

It's often said that if we knew the journey ahead of us, many of us would turn back or look for other paths. That is certainly the case here. In the great movie *Chariots of Fire*, one of my favorites, Eric Liddell, described his method of running this way: "I run the first half of the race as fast as I can and the second half faster with God's help."

Making a movie is lots of mundane work, some of it on track, some of it misguided, but it's also waiting for moments of Divine inspiration—through dreams, other people, and characters that seem to track me down, demanding to be included in the story. That's how I felt about Viktor, and, with Howie's help, he was coming to life.

9

SURFING' USA

When I first meet him, Dana Rohrabacher was a U.S. congressman from Huntington Beach, California, about twenty miles from my house. He's known as the Surfing Congressman because, well, he's a congressman and he likes to surf. Somehow, I became acquainted with Dana at a meeting of some kind and before long I found myself at his house asking him questions about Ronald Reagan. Dana knew a lot about Reagan.

When I first met him, he told me something I stored away in the vault: Reagan was never two-faced. He didn't leave a meeting and then trash-talk the guy he'd just met with. Dana knew this because he was with Reagan in such meetings and witnessed how they were before and after the guy was gone.

His house was smaller than I imagined a congressman's home would be. After exchanging pleasantries, he announced we were going to go to a local taco joint. We piled into the car and got some takeout. Back home he settled in and answered every question I threw at him about the man he clearly, to this day, adores.

Dana had so many interesting and colorful stories about Reagan—some which are so off the wall and random they just have to be true. He told me about the time when, one day out of the blue, Reagan turned to him and urged him to never cheat on his wife. Rohrabacher wasn't married at the time, but dutifully filed it away in his head for future reference. Was Reagan telling him that because he cheated on his wife? Or because he was cheated on? Or just because he wanted to warn his young friend? Dana didn't seem to know and didn't inquire further.

His life had been colorful and interesting—having worked at various times as a "journalist," fighting alongside the Mujahideen in Afghanistan, then as a member of Congress. But his driving and yet unfulfilled passion was to get his screenplay *Baja* produced.

At one time when he was down and out of money, he sold a letter that Reagan had written him offering a critique of one of Rohrabacher's movie scripts. After informing him that family films which didn't have expletives performed better at the box office, Reagan told Rohrabacher that he should get rid of all words that rhymed with "luck" and "witch."

He then told me this unforgettable story: Dana was a huge fan of Reagan in college and headed up a group called "Youth for Reagan" which was about to be disbanded. Determined to talk to his hero about it, on a whim Dana and a friend camped out on Reagan's back lawn in a tent.

The next morning, a befuddled Nancy Reagan asked them what they were doing on her lawn. When Dana explained why he must have five minutes of Reagan's time, Nancy offered a deal: it won't be five if Reagan started talking to them, it'll be twenty and that would make him twenty minutes late for everything that day.

Instead, she offered to set up a meeting with Reagan's chief of staff if they'd go home. Deal. They began to walk down the driveway toward their cars when Reagan, shaving cream covering his face, caught up to them and told them if they spent the night in his backyard the least he could do was give them five minutes of his time.

It ended up being twenty minutes—just as Nancy predicted.

But that's exactly the kind of thing that endeared Reagan to people like Dana and others. He was concerned about big issues but was never too busy to care about people. Dana returned the favor with a lifetime of devotion to the man he served in several capacities, including in the White House as speechwriter.

Dana told me another story I will always remember and learn from in my own life. Once they were on an airplane headed toward a South American country when the news came that the president of the country they were visiting was planning a devastating attack speech against Reagan upon his arrival. Dana reacted excitedly at the prospect of writing a speech wherein Reagan could attack right back and offered to begin writing immediately.

"No, Dana, we're going to do just the opposite," Reagan intoned in his soft, reassuring voice. "We're going to give a speech praising him and he'll be so ashamed that he won't be able to give the speech he was planning to give."

Dana said that's exactly what happened. It was a lesson he never forgot. Our modern discourse is littered with people attacking one another, and while Reagan was capable of strong attacks over policy issues, he also brought a gentlemanly spirit to everything he did and avoided *ad hominem* attacks. When he did attack, he often laced his comments with humor.

It was an important lesson to learn as I faced adversaries in life and a reminder that one can be both tough and gracious without compromising either. Ronald Reagan probably learned this in equal parts from Nelle and Jack—and others he met along the way.

Dana was so outlandish, so oversized, that he was exactly the kind of character our film needed, and we found a terrific actor to play him. And we re-created the famous scene of him camping out in Reagan's yard. Although I tried to coax Dennis into putting shaving cream on his face as Reagan had done, he said he wanted to do the scene without, and the shot came off perfectly.

10

LEARNING TO SAY "NYET"

I received an excited call from my pal Dave. Dave is one of those guys who more than makes up for all the bad people I've encountered in life. Just as some people are rude in a way that I don't think I deserve, Dave is a guy who is great to me in a way that I equally don't think I deserve. He is enthusiastic and easily excitable. On this day he was true to form.

"I've found a guy who is connected with a big guy in Hollywood and might want to fund the movie," he exulted.

"Great. Let's talk to him," I managed. But I've heard this before. Then again you never know. I checked out the guy on Internet Movie Database (IMDB) and learned he had a few minor credits, but nothing warranted getting too excited about him. Still, he was associated with a real bank, so I began to take him seriously.

We agreed to meet at a café in Century City. After we ordered lunch and exchanged greetings, my new friend rattled off how he was going to change the movie business by creating models that would tell him how a film was going to fare in the marketplace. He was convinced that *Reagan* was going to do well. I didn't disagree, of course. I peppered him with questions, and he answered them well. He clearly knew what he was talking about. But he was cocky. Incredibly cocky.

Which isn't always a bad thing. But it usually is.

After an hour or so he and his colleague decided we were finished so we parted ways. I was told to expect an offer. When the offer finally came, I couldn't quite make sense of it. Was he really asking for not only his share as the funder of the film, but of a huge percentage of my share as producer? Yes, my attorney assured me, it is exactly what I suspected. It's an outrageous offer, but this is business. Rather than getting flustered, I prepared a counteroffer back in the realm of normalcy.

Boy-Producer-Wanna-Be was as cocky as ever. So cocky in fact that when my attorney looked up his LinkedIn page, he discovered he had already listed himself as the producer of the Reagan movie.

His cockiness got the better of him, and he responded in a terse email that there must have been a typo because my offer was ridiculous. With that we began a several month dance of him insulting me via email and me overlooking it trying to respond constructively.

We had a middleman, Dave's friend Hank, and I often told Hank what I really wanted to say to Producer-Wanna-Be, knowing that he'd calm me down and I'd end up not telling Cocky Boy what I really want to tell him. It usually worked. In addition to the unfairness of the deal, there were also issues of control standing in the way of our consummating a deal. Cocky Boy gave in a bit on percentages.

Now, instead of taking away 80% of what should have been mine, he just wanted to take away 50%. It was an improvement but only the kind of improvement that resulted in you getting a bloody nose on the playground when you were a kid instead of getting completely pummeled. I was increasingly feeling uncomfortable with Cocky Boy to the point that even if he relented completely on the numbers, I wouldn't want to work with him.

I have two minds on this issue: Sometimes I think I just want to work with people I like. Other times I remember that life is often about working with difficult people. Still, I don't have to choose difficult people if I don't have to.

Finally, Cocky Boy and I decided to meet at a sidewalk café in Beverly Hills to fish or cut bait. It wasn't quite the Reagan and Gorbachev summit in Reykjavik, but there were moments when I asked myself what the Gipper would have done in this situation. And the answer wasn't clear, for Reagan was an enigma when it came to compromises and the art of the deal. He could walk away from a deal, refusing to budge an inch, or he could stay and make concessions that were unthinkable.

He could also offer completely game-changing compromises that made his opponents uncomfortable because of their scope and breadth. I had no such tricks up my sleeve, so I instead expressed my fundamental problems with the deal: It was a fine offer for *other* movies in other situations but not for mine. The percentage of the film I would own would be miniscule.

If I didn't think the film would do well and was just looking for a paycheck, I'd be fine with the deal. But I did, and I wasn't. I told him it was so far out of the realm of what is the norm in our business that I didn't even know how to respond. I gave him other examples of film deals and he asked me to send those numbers along to him in writing so he could review them.

I figured this was some progress.

At least he seemed to be tacitly admitting his deal was unfair. After two hours of iced tea and whatever we ate, we agreed to resume our discussion online after I got him the numbers he was looking for. As I left the restaurant, I saw a commotion on the sidewalk ahead of me. A half a dozen photographers were chasing a celebrity. As I got closer, I saw it was Kim Kardashian. I'm generally not superstitious, but perhaps this was a bad sign.

Maybe the deal was going south.

And maybe it should.

I sent along the documents Cocky Boy requested. No response. The intermediary called and told me he was waiting for me to accept the deal as is. Huh? Another round of weirdness began, and I realized I had to make a decision. I called several men whom I respected in the business. Opinions were mixed. A lawyer friend told me to take the money and run. I could make money on future deals, he assured me. This would really establish me.

Another guy said the same thing.

But I didn't feel peace about that approach in my gut. And decisions are often about the gut. I prayed, as I always do about nearly everything, but I had no clear sense of direction—except for my gut, which I guessed God gave me so maybe my gut is His answer. My attorney Jay asked me what Reagan would do. "Walk away," I said. And I made my decision.

I proceeded to tell the intermediary we're done. Except Cocky Boy decided to send me an email saying that *he's* walking away from the deal. Classic Cocky Boy. I thanked him but told him very clearly, I had made the decision to walk away but had tried again out of respect for our intermediary. Cocky Boy wrote back and, true to form, listed all my failings in the deal. I was through coddling him and responded politely but firmly that his points were incorrect and laid out what really happened. Then I thanked him and wished him the best with his ventures.

He never wrote back. The deal was over.

I've walked away. I've said, "Nyet."

Saying Nyet is very hard. It takes confidence. It takes a willingness to lose everything. At numerous points in the making of this movie I was willing to do that. I was determined to make it the way I wanted it made. No compromises on anything. That is important to me. Period.

Reagan would expect no less of me.

He modeled how to say Nyet for me, and sometimes it worked out well for him and other times it didn't—after all, saying Nyet at Reykjavik cost him control of the Senate a few weeks later. But saying Nyet is good for the soul. Besides, the idea of having Cocky boy tell me how to make my movie was too much for me to stomach.

So, Nyet it is.

11

THE DIRECTOR

I arrived early at Yamashiro, a legendary Los Angeles restaurant nestled in the Hollywood hills. I've been there several times over the years. This time I wasn't there for the food, but to meet a potential director. I won't name names, but he's a prominent director who has helmed several pictures. Not an A-lister, but a B+-lister perhaps. As you'll see, maybe there's a reason for that. He was running a few minutes late and texted me to that effect.

By the time he arrived I was on my second cup of hot Japanese green tea. After an hour or so of getting acquainted, we got down to business. I wanted him to consider directing Reagan, I told him. He had some issues with the script as it was, and we discussed how his changes could be implemented. His concerns were smart, and I was open to them.

Before we went further down that path it became apparent to me that the script was the least of our problems. He was scared. Terrified. He proceeded to tell me about a picture he had directed that was not sufficiently liberal and how he had been ordered to go back and change scenes to correct the problem. When he refused, the picture's release date was delayed by a couple of years so it couldn't provide aid and comfort to President Bush who was beginning a war right around the time this war picture was to be released.

Instead, his movie was buried and given a limited release three years later. Harvey Weinstein had decided that he would never work in film again. As a result, he was relegated to directing television, a job for which he was grateful.

All I will say about my new friend–whom I'll call Jack—is that I have never seen such a look of terror in a grown man. I tried to convince Jack he was being paranoid. If the film was a big success his career would skyrocket, I told him. He was not buying it.

"If I direct your movie, I'll *never* work in this town again," he said. Then he offered this: "I'd direct your movie if you could guarantee my income for the next ten years." We continued talking and I kept trying to convince him to change his mind. After four and a half hours it was clear I was getting nowhere. Before we parted, I asked him to at least think about it.

I relayed the conversation to Howie. "Then he's not the one," he said, telling me that the man to direct our movie needed to be as courageous as Reagan himself and not so easily intimidated. Personally, I don't think Jack was paranoid, but perhaps prone to exaggeration. Yes, Hollywood has certain collective beliefs, but I believe that often those beliefs can be overcome by the bottom line—and, if the film makes money, the objections tend to fade away.

A few days later Jack called me and once and for all begged off the project. I couldn't be angry at him. I've done similar things in my life as well. At fifteen, still thinking about acting myself, I was offered a plumb role in a sci-fi movie that could have made me a star. At twenty-two I was offered a cool job that would have been interesting and made some money. At thirty I passed up the chance to buy the house of my dreams, all decisions driven by fear. I began to emerge out of that web of fear as I grew older.

Once, my friend Martha Williamson, creator of *Touched by an Angel*, told me something I've never forgotten: "Never make a decision out of fear." I've tried to remember that. I also look back on my life and see that most of the times when I was faced with an opportunity and didn't take it, with the benefit of hindsight, I wish I had.

So, I can hardly blame Jack.

I've done what he's doing more often than I care to recount. But it was time to move on. My friends Will and Drake, actor and editor respectively, had some suggestions. One of Will's was particularly compelling. Alan Levy was a veteran of film and TV who's been directing since I was in elementary school and probably before that. I reached Alan via email on a boat in France. Turned out he was a big Reagan fan and didn't seem to be afraid of being blacklisted.

I sent him the script and he loved it. Just as Alan was looking like the one to direct Reagan, I received a curveball. I was in Atlanta at a trade show screening a movie I produced, and as I walked across the lobby I walked right past my favorite director, Randall Wallace, the man who wrote *Braveheart* and directed epic movies like *We Were Soldiers* and *Secretariat*. I understood that Reagan was a movie about the heroic, and Randy understood heroes, their faults, their strengths, and the things that motivated them. He had always been my first choice, but every time I approached him, he rebuffed me.

I didn't know him personally, so I first approached him through one of my mentors, Ralph Winter. "He's not interested," Ralph told me. A year later I spoke to his assistant and then later to his son, who told me Randy was not interested in directing other people's scripts. So, I reluctantly gave up on my dream of having Randy direct *Reagan*.

On this day, I remembered what I always tell my kids: "Joseph's never gave up." But the fact is I had given up. Then and there I decided to try again. As my daughter Anna and I took the elevator up to our tenth-floor room, I told her who I just saw in the lobby and told her to pray with me that God would give me a chance to talk with Randy.

Half an hour later, as we headed out again, we passed through the same lobby. Much to my surprise he was still there, talking with a group of people. As we walked closer to him, as surely as the Red Sea parted for the Israelites, suddenly his group began to walk away from him, leaving him standing in the middle of the lobby of the Omni Hotel in Atlanta just as I walked up to him.

I introduced myself and he was friendly and seemed glad to see me. Although we'd never met, we had several mutual friends. I quickly and half apologetically told him I was sorry to hear that he only liked to direct those films that he'd written. He quickly disagreed, saying he'd just directed *Secretariat*, a film written by somebody else. Hmmmm . . . I decided to keep pushing my luck.

"Well, you're probably busy this fall and winter when we plan to shoot," I volunteered. He didn't seem to agree with that and clearly gave the impression he was interested. We had no time to meet because he was scheduled to leave the following morning, but we agreed to stay in touch, and he asked me to contact his office. Since I didn't think I had the luxury of time, I promised to get him a script right away. So, I contacted my assistant and emailed her a copy of the script from my iPhone. Within three hours of my encounter, a copy of *Reagan* was at the front desk of the hotel waiting for Randy.

It was around midnight when I saw him sauntering through the lobby. I was at the front desk waiting for something or other and he may have had a bit to drink but was friendly as he approached the concierge. He told him he needed a new room key but had no ID on him. He offered up a copy of a book he'd just written, which had his name and photo on the back. The concierge laughed and made him his keys. I asked Randy if he got the script I left for him, and he happily nodded. I had to wonder if it was the alcohol talking, and sure enough, when I checked with the concierge my script was still at the front desk waiting for him.

He offered to have it slipped under Randy's door that night. I knew conclusively that whether he agreed to direct it or not, I'd taken my shot. I didn't mind failing. My life has been a succession of almosts. Still, I liked to at least know that I had a clear shot before I failed. And then if I fail, so be it.

For example, I wanted desperately to be a talk show host on CNN. While I was there anchoring a show for Japanese TV, I developed my own show called *Culture Clash*. At the age of twenty-six I had my shot taping a pilot for CNN. The show was considered by the top brass at the network but ultimately rejected. While disappointed, I was happy because I took my shot and didn't cower in fear. And I have a cool rejection letter from the Vice President of CNN to show for my efforts.

I didn't know what Randy would do. Perhaps another director would be "the one." But I was glad for the chance to take shots like this and keep dreams alive.

12

THE DIRECTOR PART 2

Back in Los Angeles, I asked my assistant to follow up with Randy's office as he asked me to do. When Randy's assistant asked us to go ahead and send the script, my assistant reminded him that Randy already had it. A few days later we got the response: he read the screenplay on the flight back from Atlanta and is not interested in directing.

As much as I would have liked to know his reasons why, I was glad to have an answer and to move on. And I quickly did, scheduling a lunch with Alan Levy, Ralph, and John at our favorite haunt, McCormick & Schmick's in Burbank. It's just a few blocks from where Reagan himself hung out on the Warner Brothers lot and once crashed the gates during a union strike.

Ralph was clearly unsure whether a guy with years of TV under his belt like Alan could handle a movie. John was supportive of Alan. Ultimately it would be my call. Still, I liked to know that my close friends who knew the business would be supportive of whatever decision I made. I arrived a few minutes later and the three were already seated at a table in the back room exchanging pleasantries.

Ralph and Alan have a mutual friend, one who was a

mentor to Ralph, and the conversation was easy and pleasant. Before long, we turned to question Alan about his vision of what the film should be. This is a type of make-or-break question, for though it sounds innocuous enough, it's designed to draw out the kind of director Alan might be. He gave it some thought and then told us he saw the movie as a love story.

We expected him to say how much Reagan loved his wife, Nancy. Instead, he threw us a curveball: "It's a love story between Reagan and the American people," he said, and then threw us a slider: "It's also, in a weird way, a love story between Reagan and the Soviet Union." For a split second I didn't know how Ralph and John were going to react. I was especially curious of the usually skeptical Ralph's reaction. I could tell he was intrigued by the response and eager to hear more.

Suddenly I got what Alan was talking about: Reagan's story is a love story that I've been trying to tell—and I told Alan the difference I saw between Reagan and many other politicians is that Reagan was an old-fashioned lover who woos his public as opposed to other politicians who seduce voters and then discard them after the election is over; or like other politicians who don't even bother to seduce or woo—they just have their way with the voters.

Alan had clearly passed the first test, but I was particularly interested in the way he conducted himself. One of the values I brought to the table was a desire to work with people who are passionate about their craft and who have a proven ability to get along with others. In fact, given the choice, I'd go with the slightly less talented person with a great work ethic and attitude rather than the genius who is full of himself. Like Cocky boy.

The former can grow in talent and range, while the latter can never acquire the character needed to become a good person. Alan was clearly a good person. I didn't know what his religion was or even his politics, but I could tell he always had a deep admiration for Ronald Reagan the man.

On the drive home I checked in by phone with both Ralph and John to take their pulse. They were impressed. John was sold, while Ralph was cautiously optimistic. He suggested I ask Alan for a written statement of his vision for the film. I asked Ralph what he was looking for in the vision statement and he told me that Alan, who had never directed film, should be grateful to be at the show, and should put his heart and soul into a written manifesto of what he sees the film doing.

By accident I sent Ralph's email to Alan, something I didn't discover until Alan called me. In that moment, I learned he had the character I was looking for, for instead of flying off the handle or yelling at me, he quietly asked if he should talk to Ralph and address his criticisms directly.

No, I tell Alan, it was my decision to make, and we just wanted to get your vision for the film. I thanked him for handling an indignity in such a classy way and told him perhaps it was the hand of Providence that allowed me to send that email by mistake, allowing us to get off to an honest relationship from the very beginning.

13

ANOTHER FUNDER BITES
THE DUST

Meanwhile, a former funder reappeared on the scene, offering to finance the film. One of my non-negotiables has been that I must have "final cut," which means I get the final say over content and I can market the film, something that producers typically don't ask for. From the start, this group understood this was non-negotiable with me and were fully on board.

Over the course of seven months, we negotiated and negotiated, but a strange thing happened toward the end: They began to change their terms. Suddenly, they wanted to control distribution. A month later they wanted to control marketing . . . and a few days later they wanted full creative control, something I would never agree to. Although I offered up a few compromise ideas on Friday, by Monday the deal was off.

The setback was a blow because we had come so far and had dozens of people on standby to be hired for the project. In a moment, sixty million dollars was gone—just like that. I sent my pastor Erik the email announcing the parting of our ways on the project. He wrote back: "How do you feel?"

"Numb," I replied. What I didn't tell him then was that it

caused me to ask the basic religious questions all of us ask ourselves from time to time: Is God really in this? Why would He let me go so far down this path, only to have it blow up in my face? Must I go back to my day job of helping other people's cinematic dreams come true and abandon my own?

I told Erik that 40% of me trusted in God's hand—that He has a better funding situation ahead and is in full control of the situation, while the other 60% thought I or our lawyer somehow botched this negotiation. Or perhaps it was an indication God was mad at me and punishing me for something I did or didn't do. Erik responded that he would be praying that the 40% increased and the 60% decreased, and that by the next day I'd be at 50%/50%.

I broke the news to Howie the screenwriter. He texted me back that he asked for—and received—permission from the Almighty to swear . . . and that he did so.

So, we moved on to other funders. I had a call set with Alan Levy's agent, Sam Gores, the powerful head of the Paradigm agency with whom I was supposed to discuss Alan's directing the film. Now I didn't know what to do. Should I call him to discuss a job for his client that might never happen? I had been talking to my friend Michael at Paradigm about representing me and called him for advice on how to handle the matter.

Sam's brothers finance movies, he told me and urged me to lay my cards on the table and tell Sam the truth of my situation. Later, I checked with Tom O'Malley, the president of Vivendi, our potential distributor, and he told me he was close friends with Paradigm's head of theatrical. "How did you get an appointment with Sam Gores?" he asked incredulously. Was this a Divine appointment or just another fool's errand? My call with Sam went well. I was straight with him, telling him I lost my financing for the picture. As expected, he urged me to talk to his financing guy. We set a date to meet.

14

RESURRECTION

Before I could meet with Paradigm to discuss financing, I got a phone call from John. Faithful and dependable John. He had asked me a few days earlier if I would be open to talking again with the funder with whom we'd just parted company. Sure, I replied. I had, after all, been careful not to burn bridges with them at the conclusion of our negotiations. To be sure, it was tempting to do otherwise.

On the final call I had mustered every ounce of self-control I had within me. I tried not to let on how angry I was to have been led along for nearly seven months only to be derailed at the last moment by an inexperienced negotiator and a set of demands that had never been mentioned before.

As I parked my car and prepared to climb the stairs of L.A. Fitness to begin my daily ritual on the stationary bike, I noticed John was calling me. Thinking he was calling about another film we were working on, I raised a pressing issue, and he dutifully discussed his thoughts on the matter. Then he got to the real reason he was calling: the funders wanted back in on the movie, and they've come up with some creative solutions to address our sticking points.

And just like that, the deal that was off is on again.

I wrote Erik an email: "The Lord giveth, the Lord taketh away," before adding a line that doesn't appear in the Holy Scriptures: "the Lord giveth back." For good measure I added, "Thank you for suffering through this with me."

It was indeed a perplexing turn of events, and completely unexpected, but John swore the deal was real and he'd like to negotiate it since he was close with the head of the fund. I give him the green light and he asked for a week to come back with a deal memo.

At 12:25 p.m. I wrote several members of my team, including my former intern Alex, letting them know we were back on. But Alex didn't read the email. Instead, at 3:16 p.m., thinking we were still off, he wrote to tell me that even though circumstances seemed to indicate otherwise, he was still believing that the film would come together.

I soon heard from the others as well.

"Fantastic," said Brad, one of our early supporters.

"I am super happy for you," said our future COO Tim.

"Well, this doesn't suck!" opined Howie the screenwriter as only Howie could.

Ever the sage, Ralph, who had been around the block a few times, added a note of caution: "Be careful."

I heard a TV preacher once say that God sometimes allows things to not come through until the very last moment, not out of some desire to torture us, but to remind us that it is He and not we who is in control. If that was the case here, mission accomplished. As a producer, I may think that I have things under control, but this is a poignant reminder that I do not. I was hopeful our funding situation was now intact, and I was excited to be starting pre-production. At the same time, I was ready for more twists and turns on the road ahead.

15

WITH A LITTLE HELP FROM HIS FRIENDS

I was off to speak at a dinner in San Francisco on the lessons that Ronald Reagan teaches us today. Little did I know that it is *I* who would be learning lessons about the Gipper. Before dinner, the cocktail hour was a time to mingle with the guests. I was approached by a law professor who had a Reagan story.

It was 1980, John told me, and he was a young campaign volunteer in San Diego when, a few days before the election, Ronald Reagan came to town for one last campaign swing. John had been helping candidate Reagan load and unload bags from his campaign plane. Reagan took notice and told him something to the effect that his flight out had been delayed and would the nice young man come up into the plane and have some tea and cookies with him and Nancy?

Of course, Reagan likely had no idea that he was befriending a future leader—he was just being himself.

After the speech, another man buttonholed me to tell me he had something that should be in the movie, and earnestly told me of the time in 1976 when Reagan came to North

Carolina at a pivotal moment in his race against Gerald Ford for
the GOP nomination. At a small event at a high school, Reagan
was asked what his favorite hymn and Bible verse were. The
man told me that everybody expected him to check the boxes
that most politicians check: "Amazing Grace" and John 3:16. But
not Reagan.

After telling the crowd how the members of the crew of the
Titanic had sung the song as they faced certain death, Reagan
named "Nearer My God to Thee" as his favorite hymn, and II
Chronicles 7:14 his favorite Bible verse. I thanked the man, who
had no idea of the gift he'd just given me. It's important
because the verse plays a pivotal role in the film.

Although I knew it was one of his mother's favorite verses, I
never had any independent confirmation of its importance to
him as well.

In the film, as a 12-year-old boy, Reagan recited the verse
from memory, and it showed up again during the swearing-in
ceremony when he placed his hand on his mother Nelle's Bible.
In the margins of it she had written: "A wonderful verse for the
healing of a nation."

It seemed everybody had a favorite Ronald Reagan story—
and as I heard each one, they reminded me we go about our
lives thinking that nobody is watching us, but they are. And
they will remember the idle words, the snarky comments, and,
if we're lucky, the inspirational things we have said. Most
importantly perhaps, the ways in which we treated them will
be remembered. It's not too hard to imagine that some of the
lowly people whom we've treated poorly may one day be
elevated and remember the way we really were when we
thought nobody was watching, back when they had nothing to
offer us.

One Reagan biographer is said to have grown exhausted of
all the heroic stories of Reagan treating the little man with
dignity and exulted at having finally found a man who claimed
that Reagan had once been rude to him when he, a hotel clerk

back then, checked Reagan in. But the story had a twist: the next morning Reagan came down to the clerk and apologized for his behavior the night before.

Ronald Reagan's friends—and his enemies—were watching and noticing and, nearly four decades later, still remembering.

16

PENNIES FROM HEAVEN

S hortly after Funder #2 pulled out of the film, we stepped up negotiations with another funding group that had never financed a film before. This one was especially a mystery because it was headed by a very, very young person who allegedly had access to hundreds of millions of dollars, which she was ready to put into film. I Googled her and found out she seemed to be the daughter of a billionaire hedge fund owner. If true, everything about the new funding group made sense: Dad's dollars were being used to fund movies.

So maybe, just maybe, this one was real.

I was at the Los Angeles airport in line for a decaf latte at Starbucks when I found my first penny of the day. In the next half hour before boarding my plane for Nashville, I found six more. I was traveling to Nashville to put the finishing touches on our financing for the film, off to collect a sixty-million-dollar check, which is, I think, nothing more than six billion pennies, and pennies are what I'd been finding on the ground for the last several years—along with nickels, dimes, quarters, and dollar bills, not to mention yen, yuan, pounds, and all manner of foreign currency.

I remembered it as though it were yesterday—I was finding coins on the ground every day. Finally, out of a sense of curiosity and wonder, I asked God what it all meant. Was I going to be rich? Was this a series of signs that my film would indeed be supernaturally financed? So, I asked. And waited. And listened.

I didn't hear an audible voice, but I had the overwhelming sense that I was being told the following: "The money you are finding was always there on the ground. But you never noticed it. I have opened your eyes to what was always there so that when your money does come in, you'll remember where it comes from."

I'm pretty sure those words didn't come from my brain because I'm not that articulate, but neither were they breathed audibly from on high. A religious person would say they were indeed God's words. An atheist would say I have an active imagination. You be the judge. But the fact remains that for the next fifteen years I found money everywhere—at the supermarket, in airports, on sidewalks, in every imaginable spot.

My wife was a little skeptical of such things, so whenever we were together and I'd find one, I'd show it to her. Pretty soon she wasn't as skeptical. Over those fifteen years I found nearly $700 in coins and bills and kept them in a large crystal vase. Once a year my girls and I would count that year's "earnings" and tithed on it as a reminder of whose money it really was.

So, as I traveled to Nashville collect my "check" from Funder #3 remembered whose money this was and where it came from. Human beings will do just about anything for money, and no less a philosopher than the great Cyndi Lauper has reminded us that "money changes everything."

I don't want it to change me.

We humans are such weak creatures, so prone to imagine

that we are greater, smarter, more talented, and better than we
are. Success only magnifies and contorts our already inflated
view of ourselves. Pennies from heaven are a daily reminder, not
unlike the manna that fell from the sky and fed the Israelites,
that all good gifts emanate from the Creator of the Universe.

Going to Nashville reminded me of the years working with
the band with the unusual and unforgettable name of Sixpence
None the Richer. Their name comes from a story by C.S. Lewis
in which a child borrows six pence from his father for the
purpose of buying the father a gift—leaving the father sixpence
none the richer, since in essence he was paying for, if not
buying, his own gift. I, too, consider the funding of this movie a
gift which I intend to give back, so perhaps He will then be
sixty million dollars "none the richer."

I touched down at 5:15 p.m. and had a short window of time
to travel a long distance to the party where I'd introduce my
movie to investors. With no time to spare, I rushed into the
men's room and began the transformation from jeans and t-
shirt to suit and tie.

I arrived with minutes to spare in the magnificent 20,000-
square-foot home in which the event was held. Before long I
was introduced to the assembled crowd as the producer of the
Reagan movie along with other films the group was funding.
Later I was asked to stand next to the poster of my movie and
answer questions from anybody who may wander by.

The next day, we got down to business in the conference
room of a Nashville sound stage and I was told, essentially, they
were ready to write checks as soon as we provided them with
the necessary documents. Later, as my co-producer John and I
drove to pick up my daughter Maya, who I've left with friends,
he turned to me and said, "Did what I think just happened,
really happen?"

"Yeah, I think so," I acknowledged. "But let's keep acting as
if it hasn't."

I've been disappointed so many times in the entertainment

business. So many things that were supposed to happen didn't, and so many promises were broken. Maybe I'm numb. I tend to believe things are real only when the contracts are done and the money registers in my bank. But I had the quiet confidence that this deal was finally done, that *Reagan* the movie was about to be funded and its journey to the big screen was about to be accelerated. We were ready.

At least as ready as one could be in such circumstances.

I arrived back in California enthused. I was still bothered by one detail: if these funders were so flush with cash and ready to finance a slate of half a dozen films, then why did we have to pay our own way out to Nashville for the big unveiling? Then there was the matter of the prime mover in the group being a 26-year-old. She had hired a big Nashville law firm to represent her, had leased some fancy office space in town, and was paying employees, so she seemed to be legitimate.

I was still skeptical of course. So, I researched this young woman. Her inspirational story did check out, but I still couldn't figure out how she had gotten access to so much capital, enough to fund a slate of ten movies, including mine.

My research uncovered that her father's name was a certain common Indian first name. Further, there were two options for who he was—a hedge fund manager from New York City, or a guy who ran a Kinko's in Knoxville, Tennessee. I hung my hopes on the former and traveled to Nashville. At the event I met a fellow producer, a prominent filmmaker who had produced the smash hit film *The Rookie*. Whatever concerns I had about the investor were melting away as I met other filmmakers who were also being funded by this young lady.

I tried to set aside my doubts. Lawyers worked out details and we signed an agreement. They were going to fund my movie. I was ecstatic. The worst part of the whole thing was that I had taken myself off the market. When I spoke to that group of wealthy Reagan fans in San Francisco, I had proudly declared that we were funded and had similar conversations with others.

But when it came time for funds to drop there was always a delay. I checked in often with the other producers I had met in Nashville, and they were equally confused and nonplussed. What was going on?

Howie the screenwriter had been there at the unveiling that night along with his wife who had warned him, "Something's not right about this whole thing." It was Howie who called me one day and said he had just driven past the offices where her company had been located and noticed a For Lease sign posted in the window. That was not good. And sure enough, it unraveled.

She was out of money.

That's when I remembered the research I had done. As I dug in further, she turned out to be the daughter of the guy who owned the Kinko's in Knoxville—not the hedge fund owner. I began to wonder whether she knew she would be Googled and knew that people might wrongly identify her as the daughter of the hedge fund owner and, in turn, entrust her with money and projects.

What a great scam.

And now, I was back where I started. I had lost a year in the process. Perhaps this movie was never destined to be made after all.

17

MEET THE JUDGE

Once a year we pack the kids up and drive to Monterey around the first week of October. It's a beautiful six-hour drive. After four hours or so on Interstate 5, we typically cut across Highway 46 until we reach the 101, which we take into Monterey, made famous by its most illustrious resident, John Steinbeck. The 46 is known for a more macabre event, for its where James Dean wrapped his car around a telephone pole.

It's also the closest highway to get to the amazing 6,000-acre ranch owned by the man widely believed to be Ronald Reagan's closest confidante, William Clark, better known to his friends as Judge Clark or "the Judge."

Paul Kengor, a close friend of the Judge, having written his authorized biography, urged me to visit the Judge, which I had long planned to do. Before I made the trek, I met Clark at various Reagan-related events. At a Reagan centennial celebration event, I introduced myself. To my surprise he seemed to know who I was and invited me to visit him at his ranch.

Later, at another event I again greeted the Judge and promised to visit him soon. To my surprise, a few weeks later I had a voicemail from him asking when I'd be coming up. Between five children and four movies, life was a tad hectic. Before I realized it, February has become late summer, and I still had not made the trek to learn about Ronald Reagan from one of his closest friends. Once again October rolled around, and with it, our time to visit Monterey.

It was only after I had studied the map carefully that I realized I'd been driving by Judge Clark's house unknowingly now for five years. His ranch can be seen from Highway 46 but had eluded me until now. As I turned off the 46 toward the address my GPS was directing me to, I saw on the hillside the large chapel that the Judge had built, a monument to his very devout Catholic faith.

It's an interesting historical footnote about Ronald Reagan that he was very intentionally a Protestant. His father and brother were Catholic. Although his mother had once vowed to the priest who married them that she would raise her children in the Catholic faith, by the time Ronald came around she had lapsed, and insisted on raising him in her Protestant tradition.

It's also a point of historical interest that a good deal of Reagan's close aides, like the Judge, were Catholic, and there's no doubt that Reagan's affinity for Catholics played a role in his close association with Pope John Paul II, who worked together with Reagan to throw sand into the gears of Soviet Communism.

In any event, on this day Judge Clark seemed in good spirits as I walked up the steps to his porch where he waited for me in a wheelchair. After a few minutes his two assistants who hovered briefly were gone, and he and I sat and looked out over his vast acreage, framed by a swimming pool, which I'm guessing he hadn't been able to enjoy in years. He was 80 years old now, but his mind was sharp as he effortlessly recalled events of decades before.

I brought a copy of the screenplay for him to read, but before I gave it to him, I asked if he would mind if I read him some dialogue from scenes he shared with Reagan in the movie. He nodded. I read from the scene in which Clark advised Reagan during the Iran-Contra affair that he should come clean with the American people. It's a line that came from one of those Reagan events I attended earlier in the year that featured Clark, Ed Meese, and other Reagan advisors on stage answering questions. Reagan asked Clark what he should do as the scandal threatened his presidency.

"Do what you do best," Clark recounted telling Reagan. "Tell them the truth." Clark nodded. I'd captured the moment exactly as it had happened.

On this day, Clark gave me other helpful insights. He told me something I've never read anywhere, a small factoid that's been lost to history perhaps, that he and a small group of those who served Reagan would call Mrs. Reagan "Nan-Nan." Clark told me Mrs. Reagan had a definite point of view on things and would often seek to influence her husband on policy issues as governor of California.

Reagan, Clark seemed to imply, had his own compass on most issues related to policy and charted his own course. Still, Clark would often receive a phone call from Mrs. Reagan during the time Reagan was en route to his office, and Clark was left to reassure "Nan-Nan" that he would indeed raise whatever issue she was checking in about. I got the impression that Nan-Nan and the Judge were at times on opposite sides of various issues.

History is made by men and women. Clark made history in a most unusual way by something he *didn't* do—go to the Supreme Court as an Associate Justice. The role was offered to him by Reagan himself, Clark told me, but when Clark demurred, Reagan didn't press him and turned his attention to Sandra Day O'Connor instead.

Clark was passionately against abortion. The *Roe v. Wade* decision upholding the right to the procedure was affirmed by the thinnest of margins, 5-4 a decade later, meaning that Clark's presence on the Supreme Court would have likely resulted in the procedure being outlawed.

I asked him if he had regrets about not serving on the High Court, for clearly, despite the wheelchair, had he wanted to serve he could still be shaping the jurisprudence of the nation. He thought for a moment and then said that he was needed in the foreign policy arena, and he did indeed have an impact on bringing down the Soviet Union. Then he said something I've never forgotten:

"I just wanted to get back to the ranch."

And this is why I think liberals will probably prevail over conservatives ultimately, because liberals care passionately about governing, even after they've left office, while conservatives want to get back to their ranches and their families and forget about politics. Still, I sensed regret, perhaps when his mind wandered to what that other rancher, the one from Arizona, O'Connor, did once she was put on the highest court in the land.

After an hour or so, the Judge became tired and indicated he needed to take a nap. We called for an aide, and after shaking his hand, I hopped on the back of a motorized cart driven by another aide and headed down to where my kids were playing with the Judge's horses, given to Reagan by the King of Saudi Arabia, which Reagan wasn't allowed to keep, and which had ended up with Clark instead.

Tidbits and nuggets of history are kept in the minds of men and women like Judge Clark. It's up to us to nudge them out so that we can all learn the lessons of our forefathers, to avoid their mistakes and build on their successes. Clark served his boss well. Our movie will be better because he did.

18

THE WARNING

Within Christianity there is a subset called Charismatics—not people who are charismatic in the common understanding of that term. Rather, they are those who believe the Holy Spirit inspires certain gifts—like speaking in tongues, a heavenly language that wasn't learned, getting special messages from God, and being healed of various diseases.

I'm not a very good Christian and perhaps not a Charismatic by their definition, but I do enjoy being around them. Some of them may be a little kooky, but most are very nice and smart and helpful. My friend Joe is one such Charismatic. He goes to a church called The Vineyard. And from time to time, he asked me how the film was coming along.

After another delay from a purported funder, I am perplexed. I was on a conference call where I learned our funder was closing the company, declaring bankruptcy, and was soon to start a new company.

All of this meant our project would still be funded, I was told; it had just been delayed again. I was furious and barely concealed my rage. Although I had been tempted at numerous

points to say, "I quit!" I managed to not do so. But as the implications of the call sank in after I hung up, I was more perplexed
with God than with our funder. After all, if He is in control of
the universe and owns the cattle on a thousand hills, why was
He causing this to be so difficult?

I tried to go about my days focusing on my other projects,
but I was numb and hated being asked how the movie was
going when my answer was that I was waiting for my financier
to come through.

My friend Joe didn't ask about the movie, but we emailed
about something else. Just for fun I wrote him these words:
"Something is blocking the funding of the movie. Any
insights?" I don't know what I was expecting him to write back,
but I wasn't expecting what he did write.

"Selfish ambition," wrote Joe the Charismatic. "Seriously.
That's what immediately came to mind when you asked. Maybe
at work at some level with the principals involved. Nothing
wrong with ambition, of course. I don't know if this is a word
from the Lord. It seems like it could be. But I don't know for
sure. Just reporting . . . would be worth discerning and praying
over."

Uh-oh. Does he realize that *I* am the principal?

I'm so used to warm and reassuring messages from nice
Christian people, but certainly not somebody seeming to call
me "selfishly ambitious." But he said it so nicely, going out of
his way to assure me that he could be wrong. My first reaction
was, of course, to think it must be about somebody else in the
production. Then again, this has been my baby from the beginning. If there is a problem, it had to be with me. Then I began
to parse the words "selfish" and "ambition."

As Joe had told me, ambition isn't wrong, but selfish obviously is. I don't think of myself as selfishly ambitious, but then
again, would a selfishly ambitious person be able to see it in
himself? Probably not. So, I naturally did what all of us do

when we need wisdom: I Googled. The first definition of the term "selfish ambition" turned up this gem:

> What is selfish ambition? It means to be self-seeking and always looking out for one's own interests above the interests of anyone else. The Greek word for selfish ambition is *eritheia*, and the ancient Greek philosopher Aristotle defined selfishly ambitious people as those who want to achieve political office by making themselves look bigger and better before others through trickery.

> In other words, selfishly ambitious people are those who will electioneer for office and court popular applause by deceit. They are always putting themselves forward without reference to truth. They are full of such slogans as, "Make way for me! I am better than all of you. Vote for me, and I will be your savior."

> In today's world selfishly ambitious behavior is greatly applauded. Haven't we all been told we need to look out for number one, meaning ourselves?

> In the process of seeking his own interests first and seeking to glorify himself rather than others, a selfishly ambitious person will destroy himself. Selfish ambition yields bitter fruit, in other words.

I arrived at a gas station in a sketchy part of East L.A. and, as my tank fills, I read these words on my iPhone, and they cut through my soul. "Can I really be that bad?" I asked myself. Suddenly examples flooded my mind of times when I tried too hard to promote myself. I think of my friend the rock singer who was always promoting himself in a shady way and, because he's so busy promoting himself, others don't seem to do it as much.

I see myself in him.

Everything that I do seems to be bigger than it really is.

I seem to be a successful author, but my books really haven't sold that many copies. And it suddenly hits me that maybe Joe was right. Maybe I was the one holding up the project and until I got my attitude right, the movie would continue to be held up. There's a parallel in Bible times of course, in the story of Jonah whose ship was in great turmoil.

When the crew drew straws to determine who was causing the calamity, they figured out Jonah was the problem, and if he were to be thrown overboard the storm would subside—and it did. I didn't plan to be thrown off my own project, but Joe's warning had me thinking perhaps God was trying to get my attention, that there were tasks ahead in the making of the movie that I simply couldn't do effectively until I changed my attitude and stopped being so selfishly ambitious. But how?

As any good film producer will tell you, promotion is the name of the game. We all have to promote ourselves, especially when asking investors to put down millions of dollars. But maybe I was going about it all wrong. I thought of the film conference that I was angling for a speaking slot. What if I stopped angling and just let it happen, trusting God that if it was something I was supposed to do, that He could arrange?

I thought back to *The Chronicles of Narnia* and the time I tried to act big around a certain executive, telling him that I'd read the script only to have him rage at my boss for allowing me to read it. I was trying too hard to be an important person on the film and it severely limited my effectiveness after that.

When I look back over my career most of my big breaks came from out of the blue in unexpected ways that I couldn't possibly have planned or angled for. I thought of Psalm 75:6-7 that, to paraphrase, reads, "For promotion comes neither from the east, nor from the west, nor from the south. But God is the judge: He puts down one and sets up another."

So, somewhere on the 101 freeway, I apologized to the Man

Upstairs, told Him I was sorry for being a jerk, and asked Him to promote me instead of me promoting myself. A funny thing happened. Although our check for the film didn't arrive, two days later the lady planning the film conference emailed me and asked me not only to be a panelist but to moderate the panel.

It's hard to receive correction like the one I got from Joe. But it's good for us to be humbled from time to time, especially in Hollywood where egos can rule. We all need to be reminded that we're not all that apart from Him.

19

ALTERED STATE

I was in Washington, D.C. to give a speech to a group of Reagan fans at the Conservative Political Action Conference (CPAC). I had never been to CPAC before and found the whole experience to be very educational. I soaked up every experience in the green room as I waited to give my speech, noticing the sounds and smells of everything I observed. Hollywood was old hat to me, but Washington was a town that I'd watched and read about for years but rarely experienced.

I was fascinated and transfixed. I was in Washington to speak as producer of the film on the 100th anniversary of Reagan's birth and to discuss how he affected the nation. C-Span would be broadcasting my speech live and I gave a half-decent speech for fifteen minutes or so. Later, lounging in the lobby of the hotel, I was introduced to a reporter named Jonathan Alter who has been with various publications including *Newsweek*. He had also served as a talking head on television for many years. Alter was a powerful liberal voice who had been recovering from a cancer scare.

We had a friendly chat, talking about cancer and movies. Even though I didn't consider myself a liberal, I usually enjoy their company. Come to think of it, I think I prefer the company of liberals to moderates. Liberals at least know what they believe, and I like that conviction on both sides of the spectrum.

As Jonathan and I talked he told me about a book of his that he was trying to turn into a movie. He became fascinated when I told him about my movie. Although he probably disagreed with everything Ronald Reagan stood for, he was nonetheless interested. I give my usual spiel about how I wouldn't be making it with a major studio because I'd seen what happens when studios get involved and begin to control content and distribution. He listened carefully and then said, "You *really* should speak to my brother-in-law."

"Who's your brother-in-law?" I asked somewhat cautiously.

"Michael Lynton, the Chairman of Sony," he answered.

Wow.

I didn't personally know Michael Lynton, but I was once on an email chain with him when I helped market one of his movies a half dozen years earlier. I listened to Jonathan as politely as I could but then quickly dismissed the comment. Still, I wondered what he meant. He meant something; I just didn't know what. Was Lynton a Reagan fan? A fan of presidential biographies? What was he trying to tell me? For about eighteen months I wondered but didn't do anything about it.

As our funder continued to not fund the project, I grew impatient and decided to reach out to Lynton to see if I could find the answer to my question. I revisited my email trail, found his address, and sent him a note:

Dear Michael: I'm the producer of a feature film on Ronald Reagan simply titled *Reagan*. About a year ago I ran into your brother-in-law Jonathan in Washington, D.C. at a conference where I was speaking on Reagan. When I told him what I was working on, and that I was developing it independently out of

my concern that a studio arrangement wouldn't allow me to
have the freedom I needed, he suggested I contact you anyway
and that I might be surprised.

We are in talks with independent film financiers but I'm open
to discussing the project with you if you are interested. It is a
mainstream movie intended for a mainstream audience, and a
movie that I hope will be enjoyed by both liberals and conservatives alike. As you'll see from a few of the links below, we've
gotten quite a bit of press already and we've had significant
discussions with talent. Let me know if you're interested in
discussing further.

I sent the email and waited. A month passed by with no
response. I resent the email. Bingo! This time he responded:

Mark, Many thanks for the email. Happy to talk but I think,
given the subject matter, that independent financing is probably the way to go. Best, Michael.

It's not a "Yes," but it's not a "No" either, so I responded:
"Thank you. You may be right. I would be interested in talking
with you as well. Regardless of how we are financed, I'd like to
stay in touch with you on the project as we are going to need a
strong distribution partner. Are you available for a lunch?"

"Yes," he responded, and we left our assistants to find a time
for us to get together in his office. On the appointed day I drove
onto the Sony lot, a lot full of history of a century of moviemaking. At the gate I was asked whom I was there to see. I replied
with confidence: "Michael Lynton." As I parked my car and
walked up to the receptionist, once again I was asked and once
again, I replied, "Michael Lynton." It's a good feeling. Not a
prideful feeling, but a feeling of belonging.

I arrived a few minutes early and introduced myself to

Michael's assistant and then took a seat in the area just outside of his office. Soon he walked out with his previous appointment and exchanged a few words before sauntering back into his office, this time with the door open. I pretended not to notice and kept my head buried in a women's magazine that I'm not really paying much attention to.

Within a few moments, Michael returned, introduced himself, and ushered me into his office. It was a very large office, and as I looked around, I reminded myself that this was probably the most powerful man in Hollywood, and yet he was very gracious, and seemed to be smart, open, and attentive.

I'd rehearsed what I was going to say driving down the 10 freeway. I said my prayers. And there I was. It was go-time. For the next thirty minutes we discussed the movie and my background on the other films I'd worked on. I decided to pull a George Constanza on him and give him all of the reasons why it wouldn't be a good idea for us to work together. Each time I did it only interested him more. Each time he pushed back and said he didn't agree and wanted to know why I felt the way I was feeling.

When I told him I needed to screen the film for up to a year to key leaders and that studios wouldn't allow that, he waved that off and said something to the effect that the reason studios like his don't do the same is because 25% of their movies suck. Wow. Smart and a sense of humor. I liked this guy.

That's when he dropped a bombshell on me. As we neared the end of our time together, seemingly out of nowhere, he said he voted for Reagan for president—twice. *What?* I thought. *How can this be?* I didn't want to be rude, but I am inquisitive by nature and asked him to explain.

He told me he grew up in Europe and implied that he left socialism behind and wanted to vote the other way. Twice. I was stunned. Now, I thought, I knew what Jonathan meant with the *really* in "you *really* need to talk to my brother-in-law."

Just for fun I asked Michael what Jonathan might have

meant, and he said something about his love for historical biographies. Okay. We'll let it be that. In any event, I got the chairman of Sony interested in my movie. We discussed options: If my funder came through, could they just distribute? If not, could they fund?

To both questions Michael answered yes, but that it all came down to the script. He asked to read it. I promised to send it to him. But the truth was I had a copy in my bag. Finally, after our personal chemistry was so strong, I decided that I would give it to him on the spot and not play any games. He hadn't played games with me so why should I do so with him?

But first I had to ask a hard question of him: "I'm sorry if this comes across as rude, but would you mind not spreading this script around the company and just read it yourself?" He assured me that the question was not rude and promised that only he and his assistant would read it. For some reason in these thirty minutes, I have come to trust him. I reached into my black bag and handed over the script that had consumed the last three years of my life. I was confident of it and happy to share it with him—a fellow Reagan voter.

We discussed other matters: Who will direct? I asked him who he would be looking for and he replied simply: someone who can direct. He asked what actors I had in mind. I gave him several names. He responded that the actors I suggested wouldn't do any harm to the project. He was right. I gave him a few more things to read about the project and he left me with a strangely forthright comment, something to the effect that if he liked the script, he'd like to be in business with me.

I was taken aback by the comment but did my best not to let on. There was nothing left to say so we wound down our conversation and I shook his hand and bounded out of his office, to the elevator, and toward my car.

Michael had promised to get back to me in a few days. And so I waited. As I waited, I remembered a similar meeting I had with the Vice President of CNN eighteen years earlier. I was 24 years old, just out of college and finishing my second year as a host of a TV show called *The Entertainment Report*. I had created a pilot for a talk show called *Culture Clash* and the big dogs at CNN had all watched it but decided to pass.

Still, I was exhilarated as I drove my '71 Mercedes down the 101-freeway remembering how the vice president, in turning my show down, had mentioned my name in the same sentence as the legendary CNN commentator Robert Novak. I had failed, but it was pretty cool to fail that way. This time, I was older and wiser and didn't want to fail. I wanted this deal with Sony, if the terms were right. I had the story and knew the way to market it and make box office history.

"Everybody wants to have the box office numbers of *The Passion of The Christ*," I had told Lynton. "But nobody wants to do what it took to get those numbers." And I meant it. And so, I waited for his response.

If we went with Sony, it would be because of the good graces of Jonathan Alter who stood against the political views of the hero of my story, and yet who saw a chance to help a fellow traveler on the road of life. It's a good reminder that we should never let our disagreements over issues get in the way of our common humanity.

20

WATCHING, WAITING

After the meeting with Lynton, I waited patiently for word. Meanwhile, I scheduled a meeting with the head of Lionsgate's acquisition team, Jason Constantine. I'd known Jason for several years, but we'd only done one picture together. We scheduled the meeting for a half an hour or so and at the appointed day and time I showed up at his office. I was directed to his boardroom and two and a half hours later we finished.

I spent most of the time explaining that although our movie broke many Hollywood rules, I knew what I was doing and could deliver the audience. Jason was not unsympathetic to the material or to Reagan, but his objections would likely be more practical ones: Who plays Reagan? Who directs? Those are the kinds of questions typically asked in Hollywood before all others.

Sure, there is a need for a minimum level of credibility on a movie. But if there's one thing I've learned over the last decade, it's that people are far less enamored with famous directors—or even the cast—than Hollywood thinks. Truth be told, I didn't want the latest hot superstar-of-the-moment actor or director to join me on *Reagan* because I didn't need the attitude that usually accompanies such people.

I needed an actor who would travel with me to market the film, something many actors might not be willing to do. Jason nodded and listened carefully to all of this and, like Lynton, said it's all about the script. I left a script with his name on it, and we parted ways.

For the next several weeks I wait patiently to hear from Michael and Jason. Finally, I receive a call from Steve Bersch, Michael's #2 man, who called to tell me they hadn't forgotten about my movie and were still considering it. He promised to get back to me. A week or two later I got a call from Jason who told me he had read the script and loved it—and especially the ending. Good to hear, because we labored long and hard over the final scene. I had heard the story of Reagan's getting lost while riding on his horse as his Alzheimer's progressed and how the Secret Service agent assigned to him had to tell Reagan that he could no longer ride.

It was the perfect ending to our story, a twist on the old cowboy riding off into the sunset at his moment of peak performance and strength. In contrast to this, in our film, Reagan would take one last ride off into the sunset at his moment of greatest weakness, as he read his goodbye letter for the audience. I loved this ending and never wavered from it because I felt it was the best way to counter the temptation to veer into hagiography, instead allowing for moments of weakness and humanity, and this was one of those moments.

It made me feel good to hear Jason liked both the script and the ending. But he had others in his shop to convince. He asked me if I'd come in to make the pitch to them. I agreed to do that knowing the pressure would be on. I'd have one chance to make that first impression, and the movie would live or die at Lionsgate based upon my presentation.

21

STORIES ALONG THE WAY

I n 2014, a man who claimed he attended Bel Air Presbyterian Church with Reagan told me an incredible tale. He had attended a membership class with Reagan at the church and Reagan had told this small group that he had met with would-be assassin John Hinckley to forgive him in person. I thought I had known everything about Reagan but how had I missed this incredible story? The gentleman seemed credible, so I did some digging.

At lunch with Reagan's pastor Donald Moomaw, he confirmed he had indeed required Reagan to attend a series of membership classes after the presidency, making no exceptions for his charge who had been out of town on important business for eight years. Think about that for a second. Only in America would the country's former leader be required by his home church to retake membership classes. I love so many things about America, but I love things like that most of all.

Then I checked with the former head of St. Elizabeth's hospital where Hinckley had been at the time, and he confirmed the President had called and asked for such a meeting. However, he had strongly advised Reagan not to reward shooters with private meetings and that, as far as he knew, Reagan had never followed through on it.

I further checked with Secret Service agent John Barletta who found nothing in the Secret Service logs to confirm such a meeting. He then checked with Mrs. Reagan who said it didn't happen. Could it have happened?

I suppose anything is possible. But more than likely, as Alzheimer's began to settle in, Reagan may have confused a desire to meet with Hinckley with the actual event. As much as I would have loved to have included that scene for its story-telling value, it simply couldn't be verified.

The journey to understand the man whose own biographer threw up his hands and called him inscrutable has taken me around the world, to Supreme Court Justices and fortune tellers, Prime Ministers and ranch hands, all with tales to tell of Ronald Reagan the man, not the myth. My quest to understand Ronald Reagan took me next to the Supreme Court of the United States to meet two of the Justices he had appointed, Antonin Scalia and Anthony Kennedy.

At the appointed hour I was first ushered into the offices of Justice Kennedy for a meeting arranged by his niece, who happened to be a very good friend of mine. In his carpeted chambers, with soft music playing and a butler bringing in cookies and tea, he recounted with a smile the day that Reagan called and asked him to join the Court.

"Mary and I don't know anybody in Washington," Kennedy had protested.

Without missing a beat Reagan replied, "Well, you know me!"

Kennedy relented. Kennedy then recounted the time that then Governor Reagan was visited by Hollywood heavyweights and fellow conservatives John Wayne and Charlton Heston on a mission to get Reagan to reverse a budget cut he was planning, cutting funding for the arts in public schools from $15 to $10 million.

Reagan, Kennedy said, heard them out and then gave his ruling as Kennedy looked on: he would cut it to zero and ask them to help raise the entire $15 million from the private sector. Kennedy recalled it as the worst negotiation he'd ever seen.

As we wrapped up our time together, I decided to ask him a somewhat challenging question: "What would Reagan think of your rulings?" He seemed to hesitate for just a moment and then said that overall, he thought Reagan would be pleased. I'm not so sure. Still Justice Kennedy was an invaluable source of information helping me to understand Reagan the man, as someone who knew him from his days in Sacramento.

Justice Scalia was everything Justice Kennedy wasn't and it's easy to see why they might not have gotten along too well. There's no tea service, no soft carpeting, just a down-to-earth guy who loves a good joke and a good cigar. He was so disarming that I somehow felt okay about telling him a slightly off-color joke. "I want to tell you a Reagan joke, but I feel like it may not be appropriate in these hallowed halls," I began.

"Don't worry about it," he said. "What is it?"

I recounted for him the joke that Peter Hannaford had told me. As I leaned in for the punch line, he laughed very loudly, which caused me to also laugh loudly, and as we both roared, his assistant rushed into the room.

"Justice Scalia is everything okay?" she asked.

He waved her off with a "Fine, fine." She slipped back to her workstation, unsure what had just happened.

Scalia didn't have a lot to share about Reagan, having spent precious little time with him. Still, in Scalia I sensed there was a part of Reagan there—the jovial, fun-loving ideologue. Then again, if Scalia had truly absorbed Reagan's personality, he would have attracted, not repelled, his more moderate comrades O'Connor and Kennedy, and gotten them to join him on key decisions.

I returned from Washington, D.C. and then headed to a dinner party in Beverly Hills thrown by my pal Monty Warner, a bon vivant and a man about the country. He always had interesting people for me to meet. Little did I know this evening I'd meet a fortune teller who once went to school with Reagan's daughter Patti. I pushed her for any interesting stories that might tell me more about Reagan.

The fortune teller sat to my left at a round table at the Four Seasons Hotel and her face lit up as she remembered this doozy: she visited the Reagan's home from time to time and, upon meeting Governor Reagan, she was greeted with "Are you that damn Democrat my daughter has been telling me about?"

To which she replied, "Yes, I am a Democrat."

Reagan leaned in and said, "The Democratic party is no place for a girl who's built like you." She had already told me she was a supporter of Wisconsin Governor Scott Walker, and I asked her how that had happened. She told me that a few years after that admonition from Reagan she was at a party, also attended by Senator Ted Kennedy, and the Senator spotted her from across the room and motioned to his aides that he wanted her that night. She wasn't interested and rebuffed him but remembered Reagan's warning.

A mutual friend arranged for me to meet with former Secretary of State and Reagan chief of staff, James Baker. We met on the fourth floor of my friend's film distribution company in Beverly Hills. Baker was everything I expected him to be. Smooth, with a nasal voice and Southern twang, Baker dropped this bombshell on me when I asked him if there was anything about Reagan that people might not know.

Baker told me he was in George H.W. Bush's suite when Reagan called to discuss making Bush his running mate. Reagan had just one concern: could Bush support him in his opposition to abortion? History records Bush did indeed switch sides on the issue, although his wife never followed suit. I was surprised both by the revelation and by the fact that

Baker, who was more moderate on social issues than the Reagan forces, would tell me about it.

Reagan's son Michael proved to be an invaluable source of information along the way. I first met Michael at a meeting of some kind during which he shared his life story and his conversion to Christianity. After our time together, he wrote his phone number on the back of a business card. He was at the prime of his career as a radio talk show host when we first met. Shortly thereafter, I sat across from him at Hollywood's legendary lunch spot, The Musso & Frank Grill. Michael shared several key stories that we worked into the script.

Across town pollster Frank Luntz had the coolest house and threw the best parties. His house was so massive it contained a bowling alley, a shooting range, tennis courts, and a miniature Oval Office. A few times a year he invited his friends in for one reason or another and I never missed them.

At one of Frank's parties, I ran into one of the hottest comedians of the Cold War 1980s, Yakov Smirnoff, who coined the phrase "What a country!" to describe America. When I told Yakov what I was doing he let me in on a secret: it was he who sent anti-Soviet jokes to Reagan, which Reagan used with Soviet President Mikhail Gorbachev—jokes that pointedly mocked the failings of Soviet Communism.

Reagan used these jokes to the point that Gorbachev would sometimes stop him mid-sentence to remind him that Reagan had previously shared them with him. As we stood on Frank's tennis court, Yakov seemed to take great delight in regaling me with how he helped subvert the Soviet Union and helped bring it down by giving Reagan the tools to mock it.

He got a thrill knowing Reagan was telling the jokes he, as a comedian, wasn't allowed to tell. It reminded me of the importance of comedians and entertainers being allowed to tell the truth as they see it. That conversation reminded me how quickly totalitarians will try to silence those of us who create things that impact people's lives and sometimes change their minds and hearts.

Perhaps few people knew Ronald Reagan as well as John Barletta. To better understand Reagan, I needed to soak up every ounce of time with John. We met at Judge Clark's memorial service, and as I grabbed a cup of coffee and settled in with him at a table, I got all my questions answered. Although John didn't strike me as being particularly religious, he told me Reagan *was* and that he considered his ranch an outdoor cathedral, and that he talked frequently about God. He also told me about the time he overheard two old-school conservatives, Ronald Reagan and Henry Fonda, lamenting how they both lost their daughters to the other side politically.

John was always up for a phone call, and I called him at least half a dozen times over the next several years whenever there was something I couldn't quite figure out. When we signed Dennis Quaid to play the lead role, I asked him if he'd meet us at the Reagan Ranch in Santa Barbara to give Dennis some special insights. He agreed, and as Dennis, John, and I walked the ranch, I felt something special as he gave Dennis the tools he'd later call upon to portray this most incomprehensible of characters.

John has written a book in which he described his last ride with Reagan, but on this day as the three of us stood in Reagan's small adobe on the ranch, I asked if he would tell us the story one more time so that Dennis could hear it. John obliged and reminisced.

Six months later, John was dead, felled by cancer, but his story lives on in us.

On the set I told the story exactly as it happened to our actor, Trevor Donovan, and then arranged for him to speak to John's sister in Boston. She asked if he'd be doing John's slight Boston accent. Trevor graciously agreed to do so, spending the next twenty-four hours getting that accent just right. I'll be forever grateful to Trevor for that.

What I especially enjoyed in meeting Reagan's old pals were the stories lost to history that tumbled out of them—the things they forgot to put in their autobiographies or tell the historians.

In 2015, I traveled to Tokyo to meet with former Prime Minister Yasuhiro Nakasone, Reagan's counterpart in what would come to be known as the Ron-Yasu relationship. Reagan and Nakasone were both right-wing ideologues. Both came to power around the same time, 1981 and 1982. I had an hour or so with Nakasone and he shared his remembrances of Reagan in very personal terms, unusual for a Japanese leader.

Nakasone described Reagan as a "Leader of leaders," referring to Reagan leading the group of Western democracies that had come to include Japan. Nakasone recalled the time he told Reagan he would be the catcher to Reagan's pitcher, then slyly reminded the President that sometimes the pitcher needed to go along with the catcher's signals for the pitch to throw. Reagan agreed. Nakasone, thrilled to have the President visiting his home in the countryside, dutifully installed a Western-style toilet so Reagan wouldn't have to squat in a Japanese-styled one.

From Will Sadleir, another former Reagan aide, came the revelation that it was M&M's—not the widely publicized jelly-beans—that were Reagan's favorite candy. He also told me an incredible story of how Mrs. Reagan had called him to request a schedule change for their return trip from Washington to Los Angeles. Sadleir had asked to keep the schedule as it was because he had a Boy Scouts meeting he hoped to keep.

A few weeks later, the future First Lady called to thank him for not making the change. The flight she had proposed as an alternative crashed in Chicago and all passengers aboard lost their lives.

But perhaps the most impactful of all of my encounters was meeting the man himself. I got the idea that I might be able to get in to meet President Reagan when one of my friends was able to arrange for a meeting.

Summoning up my courage I wrote a letter to Reagan's chief of staff asking if I could meet the President. I decided to bring out the big guns by telling her in my letter than I had once violated federal election law when in 1980 I punched the hole in my Father's absentee ballot for Ronald Reagan. And just like that, a few weeks later I received a phone call asking when I might be able to come in for said meeting.

As we worked to find a date she suddenly said that a cancellation had just come in and could I make it tomorrow. And just like that, 24 hours later, I was ushered up to the 24th floor of the Die Hard building in Century City. I would learn later that the person in charge of my encounter was Peggy Grande who became a friend many years later.

As Peggy ushered me into Reagan's office I noticed that she had a sing-song quality to the introduction as though she was talking to a child. "Mr. President, Mark Joseph is here to see you!"

And there he was. I could tell immediately that he wasn't all there and it created a moment or two of awkwardness. Realizing that I'd have to carry the conversation I pointed out to the street below and said something like, "You have a beautiful view of the city."

He turned his head but looked blankly back at me. I tried to take in all the sights in his office but within a few moments Peggy was back offering to take pictures. And then before I could say much else to him our time was coming to an end as Peggy gestured that it was time to wrap things up.

Suddenly I was filled with regret—I had met him but we hadn't really connected. So as I walked toward the door of his office, I decided to turn around and give it one more shot. "We all love you very much Mr. President," I blurted out awkwardly and, to my surprise, he came alive for the first time that day, and winked at me.

Of course I had no idea I'd be one day making a movie about him, but even that short encounter helped give me a measure of the man that would help years later as I worked to flesh out the character. Reagan was not as tall as he had been of course, but as we charted out his last horse ride in the film, that reminder of his physicality in those waning days would guide us as we prepared Dennis for the last horse ride in the film.

22

THE CHAMP

There are a million reasons why I know that God has a sense of humor. Among these are the fact that I, forbidden from attending movies as a child, am a movie producer. Another is that I had lunch with Jon Voight to discuss his playing an important role in the Reagan movie—the same Jon Voight who I was whisked away by a sympathetic big brother to watch in a movie called *The Champ* when I was 11 years old, all behind my strict parents' backs of course.

I had worked with Jon on a film called *Holes*, but we had never met until a few years back. Although neither of us is Mormon, we had attended a Mormon-based awards show honoring the best movies in Hollywood for that year. After the show we struck up a conversation as we waited for the valet to bring us our cars. All I remember from that evening is he asked who I had in mind to play Reagan. After I rattled off a few names, he mentioned he might be interested in playing the role. Although I had James Baker, Reagan's chief of staff, in mind for Jon, I remembered the conversation, for it's not every day an Academy Award–winning actor makes such an offer.

I kept in touch with Jon and, a few weeks later, invited him to a screening of another film I was working on. The topic of Reagan came up again. He was 74 at the time and I'd need someone who could play Reagan from 40 until the end. Jon just didn't seem right for the part. So, I mentioned the character of Viktor, the KGB agent who plays a lead role as the film's narrator and storyteller.

We made a lunch date to further discuss the film. I brought my director Alan and co-producer John along for the lunch at one of my favorite hangout spots, The Farm.

We lingered for nearly four hours. Jon is great company. Finally, we got down to business. Jon had visited Russia and said something I will never forget: It's all in the eyes. He had visited the Soviet Union when it was under Communist control and once again after the USSR had been dismantled. He noticed how the eyes of the people were different.

It's been said the eyes are the window to the soul, and that's what Jon found. Soviet eyes were dead and avoided direct contact with others. Russian eyes engaged and were alive with human emotion. Then Jon added a twist: What if Viktor still held out hope that Russia might defeat America, as America moved toward totalitarianism and Russia continued down the path to freedom?

Jon's experiences in the Soviet Union reminded me of the words of another actor, Marion Ross, of *Happy Days* fame. I had grown up watching her play "Mrs. C" on the show and one day found myself talking to her at the birthday party of my friend Martha Williamson.

Mrs. C had also visited the Soviet Union, and when I told her I was working on a movie about Ronald Reagan, she regaled me with a story of her visit to the Soviet Union on a mission's trip with her church. While she didn't notice the eyes as Jon had, she had noticed menacing pictures of Ronald Reagan on the streets of Moscow. One was a grotesque painting of Reagan as a monster-like bird with talons and an angry scowl that haunted her to that day.

Actors like Jon and Marion are our storytellers, and their memories helped me to shape the story, ensuring it reflected the world they saw, as only storytellers can.

With Dennis and Mena Suvari. Mena was two months pregnant when she delivered an amazing performance as Reagan's first wife Jane Wyman.

At the Reagan Ranch preparing Dennis for an outdoor scene.

Prepping for a scene in the Oval Office.

Dennis and I confer as he prepares to go on the last horse ride that ends the movie.

Catching up with John Barletta, Reagan's favorite Secret Service Agent.

Ed Meese gave us behind the scenes insights.

TOP: In Jon Voight's office as we rehearsed lines.

ABOVE: Visiting with William "Judge" Clark at his ranch in Paso Robles, California.

LEFT: We announced the casting of Dennis at the Reagan Ranch on the Today Show with Megyn Kelly.

With my team that brought Reagan to life on the last day of our California shoot: Howie Klausner, Sean McNamara and John Sullivan.

ABOVE: Dennis's mother passed away shortly before we began shooting but mine joined us and offered a prayer the night before we began shooting.

RIGHT: In the studio with Gene Simmons recording the classic song "Stormy Weather."

TOP: John Avildsen, David Henrie, Paul Kengor; LEFT: Conferring with David Henrie. COVID delays pushed his part of the shoot back nine months; RIGHT: On the set in Guthrie, Oklahoma.

Dennis and I on the red carpet at Hollywood's famed TCL Chinese theater in our matching tuxes.

Filmmaking in the era of Covid.

Jordan and I watching Dennis deliver Reagan's Berlin Wall speech.

On the road at a trade convention selling the movie.

A serious moment in the studio.

23

GONNA FLY NOW

Who would have thought that finding a director was such a difficult task? Of course, in any normal situation it's not. But this movie needed a special director—one who understood he or she wasn't the star of the story. Far too many directors unfortunately have come to believe they are indeed the star.

Who can forget the words of Darren Aronofsky, when challenged with the information that his film on the life of Noah wasn't testing well with religious audiences? He famously declared he was above test scores. Seriously? None of us are above being evaluated by our bosses or our customers.

Then there was the Narnia director who seemed to think the beloved children's series was his story—not C.S. Lewis's— and acted that way.

Anyway, despite my great affection for Alan Levy, it had become apparent we needed to find another director. I came to enjoy our phone calls and meetings, but my potential financiers made it abundantly clear they simply couldn't get financing if a TV director with no experience in film was at the helm.

I fought long and hard to keep Alan, but reality set in, and I realized we had to make a change. So, I made a lunch date with Alan. He was a veteran and a pro. As we sat down to lunch, he said something like, "Let me make this easy for you: I know why we're here."

We spent the rest of the meal reminiscing and catching up on our lives. Alan remains one of the classiest guys I know in Hollywood. He has directed some of the greatest TV shows in my lifetime and has great instincts. Our need to move on to another choice had nothing to do with skill or expertise. Rather, it had everything to do with the way Hollywood is organized.

The way things are done in tinseltown is that films are financed by professional financiers, number crunchers really—and not artists. The numbers they crunch have to do with what an actor or director has done in box office sales in the last five years. Period. Alan had no box office in the last five years or the last fifty years and that's that.

The decision to proceed without him left me with no idea where to turn next for a director. In a moment of frustration, I reached out to Ralph. For fifteen years I had reached out to Ralph in moments like these. In movieland, he is my big brother. Always dependable and steady, that's Ralph.

I explained my dilemma. His answer was deceptively simple and offered in the form of a question: "What's your favorite movie?" I thought for a moment of all the great movies I'd seen.

"*Rocky*," I answered.

"Okay. Then go find the guy who directed *Rocky*."

Hmmm. Simple yet brilliant. "OK," I told Ralph. Although I'd watched *Rocky* probably a hundred times in my life, I had no idea who the director was but quickly discovered his name was John G. Avildsen, and yes, he was alive. I reached out to his manager. She appeared grateful for the call and asked for the script. Months passed with no response. When I followed up with her she told me he had read it and loved it.

We arranged to meet, the three of us, but she had a flat tire. Just John and I were able to make the meeting at a small café in Beverly Hills. John was short in stature with a solid crop of hair and an intense look that gave way to an easy smile after a few minutes of casual conversation.

I was careful not to tell him what *Rocky* meant to me. I didn't want to appear to be too much of a fan-boy. But that film played a large enough role in my life that in my high school yearbook one of the three words used to describe me was "Rocky." I don't think it's an exaggeration to say that among other influences, John's movie taught me how to be a man.

I grew up in a feminized and feminist culture in which it wasn't clear how to be a man. By contrast, Rocky was strong yet kind, determined yet nonchalant. For a while I even bounced a ball around as I walked down the hallways of my high school— just like Rocky did.

John shared great stories about how the film was made. He only had $900,000 to make it, he said, and that required constantly doing things to save money, which turned out to be brilliant. Rocky and Adrian were originally scheduled to have a date at a restaurant, but for creative reasons and to cut costs, John suggested an ice-skating rink instead.

But when they found one, renting it proved to be far too expensive. So, he asked if they could come after hours. The owner agreed. And so was born one of the greatest date scenes in cinema, the overeager Rocky and the reticent Adrian, her skating on the ice and him walking alongside.

John shared great stories about his almost directing *Saturday Night Fever* and being thrown off the picture. He told me about his upbringing in Illinois and how he came to Holly-wood. I was increasingly feeling like John was the one. He is known as the "King of the Underdog" and has had documen-taries and books made about his prowess.

One problem. He hadn't worked on a major picture for many years. I knew that if I chose John, I would have more struggles ahead. And yet I knew it would be easier with John than with Alan because he is a film director—one who has won an Oscar no less. After lunch I promised to be in touch.

A few nights later I happened to be having dinner with a small group that included the Executive Editor of the *Hollywood Reporter*. I asked him, "What is your opinion of John Avildsen?" His reply was quick and clear.

"He's the greatest director this town has ever produced."

Wow. That was the reassurance I needed. John is our man.

Working with a living legend like John Avildsen was mostly a joy, but also occasionally challenging. The joys outweighed the challenges by far. I savored every moment we spent together, remembering that he wouldn't be around forever, and the stories he was telling me would likely be lost to history if I didn't remember them.

Over lunch one day with Howie and John, we peppered Avildsen with all our Rocky questions, and he didn't disappoint. Another lunch found John and me, author Paul Kengor, and the actor who agreed to play young Reagan, David Henrie, at the table.

Avildsen was a repository of film knowledge, but he also became my teacher about life. One day at lunch he said something so profound I immediately grabbed my iPhone to write down his words: "You can't worry about losing face if you're doing it for the right reason because the principle is greater than your pride."

I don't recall what we were talking about that prompted him to utter this nugget of wisdom, but it probably had something to do with the great challenges we had faced in making this movie.

John's contract took awhile to negotiate—sometimes I joke that John's team negotiated as if it was 1977—but it wasn't 1977 and many of my Hollywood friends couldn't figure out why I'd want to work with John. All I can think about are the amazing ads we'd run that will say, "From the director of *Rocky* comes

Reagan." Not to mention there's something magical about the genius that comes with age.

I was born and raised in Japan by Americans living there and that likely explains my deep respect for my elders. And John is an elder. So much so that there's real concern as to whether he would be able to pass the physical required by a bonding company. He finally agreed to take his physical and we agreed to terms.

John G. Avildsen, the living legend, would be directing my movie.

24

THE OTHERS

I broke the original story about our film in 2010 in *The Hollywood Reporter* not because I wanted the news about our movie to be public *per se*, but simply because I wanted to beat another Reagan movie to the punch. A few years later I learned about another movie called *The Butler*, which portrayed Reagan in a rather unflattering light. Although I wasn't particularly concerned about a film that merely featured Reagan but wasn't *about* him, nonetheless I had to monitor it carefully.

When we first started getting messages on our Facebook page objecting to our (allegedly) having chosen Jane Fonda to play the role of Nancy Reagan, I was mildly amused. There were angry calls for boycotts, heartfelt pleas that we change our minds, and the occasional expletive from furious Vietnam veterans.

At first, we attempted to set the record straight. "Wrong movie," our Facebook team would write back. "You're thinking of a movie called *The Butler*." But in time, the trickle turned into a flood, and it seemed that no amount of attempting to set the record straight would stop the misunderstanding. And that was before the movie was even released.

When *The Butler* hit theaters, the controversy sharpened as filmgoers saw a fictionalized account of Ronald Reagan and his relationship with the central character of the film, the White House butler, Eugene Allen. On the big screen, Allen's character quit his position not long after his apparent disgust over Reagan's refusal to support sanctions against South Africa and, after feeling like a prop at a state dinner, he was invited to be a guest of the First Couple, then joined his son at an anti-Reagan protest.

There was also a critical moment in the film when President Reagan pondered aloud to Allen whether he had been on the wrong side of civil rights. In real life, Allen "was especially fond of the Reagans," as reported by the *Washington Post*.

A good friend of Allen remembered, "He often talked about how nice they were to him." Away from Hollywood make-believe, there was no mention of why Allen chose to retire from his three decades of service as White House butler, other than that it was time. And in real life, Allen marveled to his wife how they got to enjoy the champagne he once served—thanks to the Reagans' invitation.

Across the political spectrum, historians, biographers, and former Reagan aides condemned the movie's caricature of Reagan as historically inaccurate and personally unfair, many noting that the president didn't have a racist bone in his body and was remarkable in his personal sensitivities toward minorities. As expected, while film critics praised the film, if our Facebook page and the reaction of other prominent Reagan biographers were any indication, there was palpable anger over what was perceived to be an ideologically driven attack on Reagan.

While I wasn't too concerned about *The Butler* encroaching on our territory, I was concerned about another movie, *Reykjavik*, with Michael Douglas attached to play the role of Ronald

Reagan. While I knew this film would never be a hit with Reagan fans with a casting choice like that, it could nevertheless make our lives difficult in attracting investors to our script.

Casting Douglas as Reagan was a classic Hollywood miscalculation, the types of choices made every day by people out of touch with the heartland. I happened to mention what had transpired to a reporter friend at *U.S. News & World Report* who subsequently wrote a story chronicling the unique challenges this casting choice faced in a piece entitled "Michael Douglas Should Not Play Ronald Reagan." The reporter noted:

> Done right, with a script that holds to the actual history and not some post-historical fantasy of moral equivalence, it could be a hell of a picture. In fact, it would be the kind of picture that Reagan himself might have starred in during his own Hollywood days—as the hero, the gritty American, the one man who sees the truth, the loner holding out against all odds for what is right. The kind of role that, in an "A picture," went to Gary Cooper, Jimmy Stewart, John Wayne, or Randolph Scott.

> Instead, Reagan is going to be played by Michael Douglas who, while not a bad actor, is not exactly the kind of guy one immediately thinks of as presidential material even though, as mentioned, he played one in a Hollywood liberal fantasy about what Bill Clinton ought to be and how he should really act. . . . Douglas, like many of his colleagues who were in front of the camera in the 1980s, had nothing good to say about Reagan, nothing at all.

What the writer didn't note was that Douglas had lent his name to a group called "Hollywood Concerned" back in the summer of 1984. He also organized an anti-Reagan group of celebs who raised money to support Reagan's nemesis in Nicaragua, the Communist leader Daniel Ortega.

From my vantage point, the piece was a devastating blow to *Reykjavik,* and it lingered around for many years until, after we had completed the first part of our shoot in 2020, it was announced that the film would indeed be made, but not for the theaters but rather for a streamer. I was relieved. A streaming series about Reagan starring Michael Douglas was no threat to us.

Then there was the saga of poor Will Ferrell.

In late April of 2016, Ferrell announced he was going to star as Reagan in a black comedy featuring the comedian playing the President as a man so captured by Alzheimer's disease, he had to be convinced that he was playing the President in a movie role in order to get him to function. Reaction against the film was swift and powerful:

"Alzheimer's is not a joke—it kills—you should be ashamed," Reagan's son Michael tweeted, while his daughter Patti wrote, "Perhaps for your comedy you would like to visit some dementia facilities. I didn't find anything comedic there, and my hope would be that if you're a decent human being, you wouldn't either."

Our Facebook page lit up like a Christmas tree again and I noticed a posting from one individual who urged fellow Reagan fans to call Ferrell's alma mater, University High School in Irvine, California, and ask the school to remove Ferrell's name from the wall of fame. They included the school's phone number. Even I was surprised by that one.

It took Ferrell all of two days to recant his involvement: "The Reagan script is one of several scripts that had been submitted to Will Ferrell which he had considered. While it is by no means an 'Alzheimer's comedy' as has been suggested, Mr. Ferrell is not pursuing this project."

Such was the lame attempt at damage control by his camp.

25

WILL THE REAL REAGAN PLEASE STEP FORWARD?

The first question I usually got about the movie was "Who's gonna play Reagan?" I heard it a thousand times. And although I was known to rattle off some names, the truth is I just didn't know. Early on, I considered Jim Caviezel, the actor who had played Jesus in *The Passion of The Christ*.

Although I had worked on the film producing the rock soundtrack and doing marketing for it, I had only briefly met Jim and found him to be a bit distant. When we finally met for lunch at Bob's Big Boy in Burbank, he was *intense*.

As I explained the film to him, he told me how he had memorized entire Reagan speeches and proceeded to recite one, Reagan's famous 1964 speech. I later had lunch with his lawyer Frank, and we agreed to keep in touch. But when Jim's TV series *Person of Interest* took off, his shooting schedule made it almost impossible to be in our movie.

In the meantime, everybody on my team had an opinion about who should play Reagan. One suggested Gary Oldman who they had worked with recently. I didn't know Gary, but I was introduced to his manager Doug, and we went to lunch at my favorite spot in Beverly Hills, Caffe Roma. The meeting was positive and upbeat, but I just didn't know if Gary was the right person.

For starters he was considerably shorter than Reagan and he didn't seem to have that cowboy gait. When I learned that he agreed to play Winston Churchill I was even more skeptical. But some members of my team insisted Gary would get us financed instantly, so we made an offer to his agent. We didn't hear anything back. I was relieved. At the gut level, I didn't think he was the right person for the role.

So, it was back to Caviezel.

I've worked on several of Jim's movies, but I've never produced a film for him and for some reason we had a hard time connecting. Once, at an event, I greeted him and, as we spoke, I noticed he was looking over my shoulder and then, suggested I should be in touch with one of the men who produced one of his previous movies to discuss Reagan. That was sort of like asking a girl out on a date only to have her refer you to an ex-boyfriend. But I made the offer to his agent anyway and then waited.

I've learned the hard way to be flexible on these types of issues and to listen to the voices of those around me and watch the hand of Providence guide through events. I met Jim's manager Beverly several years back and she was ecstatic about him playing the role.

But she developed Alzheimer's and stopped managing him. I was left to deal with his lawyer—whom Beverly had warned me was never enthusiastic about these types of projects. Jim's lawyer and I had lunch in a quiet outdoor patio restaurant in Beverly Hills and agreed to keep in touch. Shortly after I made the offer to his agent, his lawyer passed away, and his agent didn't seem too enthusiastic. On top of all of that, Jim himself continued to be oddly evasive. I reached out to him through

Will, one of his best friends, who was a big fan of our film. Even with his endorsement Jim seemed noncommittal.

So, I waited but got no clear answer from his agent.

These circumstances made me think that a door was shutting despite my best attempts to push my way through it. So, I gave in and stopped pursuing Jim. We had discussions with agents who represented other actors. I thought Kyle Chandler might be an interesting choice and reached out to his agent as well as to my friend Ned who knows Kyle's wife.

I got the usual noncommittal response from the agent, and through Ned it seemed that although Kyle's wife wanted it for him, Kyle didn't show interest.

While at the Reagan Library and Museum for the 2016 GOP presidential debate, I sat near a talent agent friend who rep's various actors including Charlie Sheen. We talked Reagan and he suggested Charlie for the role. Not the right fit, I said, but then asked who else he represented. He mentioned David James Elliott, the star of the TV series *JAG*.

His suggestion resonated with me. I figured that Elliott could be an interesting choice for Reagan for several reasons. David is tall and Reaganesque. He's the star of the *JAG* but hasn't had a breakout film role yet.

"Perfect," I said to myself.

But would he be interested?

My agent friend asked David and was told yes. A meeting was quickly arranged, and David and I met for coffee at a new-agey coffee shop in Brentwood. I was blown away by David—I was intrigued with the idea of taking a less-than-famous actor and letting him become the character so that viewers wouldn't be distracted by the actor and could really believe he's Reagan.

We came to terms with his agent on the fee and made arrangements to travel to the Reagan Ranch for shots of David as Reagan. He put on the cowboy hat that I got from the Reagan Library gift shop and put his feet up on the very table where

Reagan had once done so in front of his house. The resemblance was uncanny. We've found our man. Or so I think.

Now all that was left was to convince my director, John Avildsen. He was open to the idea but wanted to meet David. Fine, I said. But then he mentioned he'd like to have David read for him, something not all actors feel comfortable doing, and David's manager made it clear to me that David did not want to read for John, as though he's auditioning for the part.

David wanted to meet once he'd been selected. I explained this to John's manager who promised that John wouldn't ask David to read. I assured David's manager of the same. So, lunch was set up at Caffe Roma, but for some reason I had a sick feeling in the pit of my stomach that day. I had a tough job to make sure my potential star and my potential director could get along well enough to make this amazing movie.

We sat, David to my left and John to my right, and made small talk. David was incredibly gracious—he had watched some of John's movies and John was flattered. We ordered lunch and things went smoothly until John asked David, to my horror, that he'd like to have him read for him some time. David looked at John and then looked at me; he was not pleased. A few awkward seconds later David announced he had to leave. He stood, shook our hands, and walked away.

This was not good.

John and I parted ways, but not five minutes passed before I took a furious call from David's agent who was screaming at me. I was certain that my life in Hollywood was over. David is off the project, he barked, and now I was stuck with an 81-year-old director and no lead actor. It was shaping up to be a long Christmas season.

I reached out to others along the way. I spoke to Christian Bale's agent who said Christian read the script but "didn't understand the character." Mel Gibson's manager read the script and said that, even though he's a liberal, he still loved the script, but Mel wasn't interested. Greg Kinnear's agent wasn't interested.

Then I had a conversation with Nicolas Cage's manager who said Nic was interested. And so began a strange odyssey that to this day has me slightly baffled. A meeting was arranged in Las Vegas for me, my co-producer, and Nic. We arrived at a hotel restaurant in town and checked in, asking for the table where "Dr. Blue Jay" might be. He was sitting close to the window—and we soon discovered he was a very friendly fellow. We had a nice long discussion about Reagan and the role. We never discussed politics, but I did have a sense that he's a middle-of-the-road apolitical type perhaps, which was great for me.

The staff liked Nic a lot and he was friendly and generous with everyone—taking photos with a fan. He revealed his girl-friend is Japanese. When I told him I was fluent he put her on the phone, and we had a nice chat. We agreed on all details, and driving back to Los Angeles, it looked as though we were going to make the film with Nic.

To be clear, he was not my top choice, but by this time I just want to make my movie and was willing to make some compro-mises. He was very financeable—meaning other countries would pay us advances of amounts they projected the movie could make based on his track record. I figured with enough hair and makeup we could pull it off. I reassured myself he's an A-list actor, which meant whatever he might lack in natural Reagan looks he could make up for with his acting ability.

Nic and I communicated by phone and text. He was unfail-ingly polite and gracious. I burned lots of Reagan DVDs containing speeches and movies and sent them to him to review while we began the work of getting our investors together. We planned to shoot in 2017 and, as 2016 wound down, I was making plans to take my bi-annual family vacation to Japan.

On the morning of our departure, the family was packed in

the van. I was just getting ready to drive away when I got a text from one of my consultants who asked me if I'd seen a story in the *New York Post* about Nic. I said, "No," then hung up and quickly searched for the story.

To my horror I found the piece:

> Nicolas Cage is wondering whether the role of Ronald Reagan would damage his career. The Oscar-winning actor has been offered the lead in a movie that will show the conservative president in a flattering light, infuriating the liberal Hollywood crowd—the opposite of "Reagan," the movie in which Will Ferrell was going to play the president as senile. Cage's publicist Stephen Huvane declined to discuss the new movie. "It's way too early in the development process," he said.

This was not good. In fact, the article was very bad news. My kids and all the luggage were in the mini-van ready to go, but I couldn't go to Japan with this hanging over my head. I went for a walk with my cellphone and quickly tracked down his manager and asked if this was leaked by his camp.

He swore it wasn't and that Nic was still excited.

I wasn't so sure.

But since we were headed into the holidays, I hoped maybe the article wouldn't be noticed. So, I took the trip feeling assured. When I got back a few weeks later, Nic and I met for lunch at the Regent Beverly Wilshire, and he assured me that all is well and he's not worried about any reaction from Hollywood. I felt better. My father had just passed away, and we talked about his father and how he had promised to scatter his ashes in Italy and how he carried the urn on a plane to accomplish that mission. With Nic firmly committed, we got to work.

That's when the hard work of convincing my director began.

As I said, John is a legend and I wanted to defer to him as much as possible, but some of his casting choices were, well, from a different decade—the 1970s to be exact. He really wanted John Travolta for the role. I have great respect for John, but just didn't see him playing Ronald Reagan.

Taking a different tack, I ran several names by him— including my favorite, Dennis Quaid, whom he liked for the role. I had always pictured Dennis in this role and had heard through the grapevine that he had told a mutual friend that he might like to play Reagan. So, I sent Dennis a message through this friend only to hear back that Dennis had said that any conversations about the role should happen with his agent.

I took that as him not being particularly interested. But while he liked Quaid, John was dead set against Nic Cage for all the reasons you think he might have been. I tried to reason with John that I understood his feelings but that we should at least take a meeting with Nic to see if John could get comfortable with him.

John agreed and Nic was ready to meet, but to my surprise, the day before our scheduled meeting at the Regent Beverly Wilshire, John pulled out. I was nonplussed. I loved John and wanted to work with him. But his refusing to even meet was a bridge too far. I had to do something very difficult, and unthinkable: fire my hero, the man who made one of my favorite movies of all time.

I thought about it for a day before I informed his manager that I was letting John go. She immediately wrote back after we spoke explaining John's strong feelings about Nic: "Please understand. John's logic in not attending the meeting was he felt it would be a dishonor to all of you as he was so adamant that he was not right for the role. He simply did not want to waste anyone's time. He should have played ball and attended; I felt like I failed in making that happen."

She added, "I don't think it's any secret that John can be quite stubborn at times! You need to know that he did and does want to direct this film. That has never been the issue. I totally understand your decision, you have been more than patient.

However, we have all worked so hard on this, and I can't give up! I just need to throw a Hail Mary at you. John loves the idea of John Travolta. He thinks he would be terrific! If I had John personally talk him into it, we could bring Travolta to the table, could this be salvaged? Just a thought, as I'm heartbroken this has not worked out."

Now I was left with an actor but no director and simply didn't know what to do next. I informed Nic's manager that I had to let our director go because of the circumstances and asked if Nic had any suggestions for a new director. He had none and preferred to leave that decision up to me.

On a hunch I thought about a director that I knew Nic recently worked with on another picture. I was ready to make the offer to him, when Nic's manager told me he was less than enthusiastic about that director. I remembered another director who had been on my radar: Sean McNamara, who made the leap from television to film with the film *Soul Surfer*. I explained the situation to Sean, and he readily agreed to take on the project if Nic was agreeable. Over the holidays, Nic thought about Sean directing. I was thrilled when the word came back that it was a "Yes."

So now I had a director and a lead actor, which meant we're all set to move forward. Sean joined the meeting in Las Vegas, and we seemed good. Until one day, a few months later, when completely out of the blue, Nic's manager called to say, without explanation why, that Nic just didn't want to do the project. I pressed him for answers but didn't get any.

He was cordial and friendly, but I really don't know to this day what happened. Was the *New York Post* story, right? Did I scare him away with all my DVDs I sent to him? I'll never know. But in my game of musical movie chairs, I now had a director, Sean McNamara, and no talent.

Why didn't I become a dentist or an accountant?

Sean is a mensch. His background was in TV, which meant his ego was minimal and he knew how to work fast. He promised to stay engaged even though I had no lead actor. And now it was back to the drawing board. I was reminded of my first choice for this role, Dennis Quaid. Sean directed Dennis in *Soul Surfer*, so that was a plus. I decided to make an offer to Dennis's agent.

One week went by, no answer. Two weeks, still no answer.

Finally, we reached out and were told he was passing on the opportunity. What to do? My friend Noah, the brother of Bethany Hamilton, promised to talk to Dennis about the role and when he did, Dennis said he never heard about the offer. He was indeed interested and, although talks with his agent dragged on for another six months, at least we were in the ballpark.

But Dennis still wasn't convinced he could play this part, so we arranged for a dinner in Malibu to discuss his concerns. I decided to meet at my friend Dick Riordan's restaurant, Gladstone's, and arranged for us to dine in a quiet back room but only after enlisting my "road pastor" Michael Guido to pray for our meeting. Guido, as he's affectionately known, ministers to rock stars and movie people like me—a sort of preacher without a church.

Dennis and I were to meet at the same restaurant that I met Dick at two years earlier when he was considering putting $5 million into the film. Dick is the former mayor of Los Angeles and an all-round nice guy. Probably the last Republican Los Angeles will ever see as mayor. I'd once had him on my television show back in 1994 and we've had dinner a few times over the years. When we had dinner at Gladstone's, investing in Reagan was on the table. I gave him my best pitch of why the country needed the movie and he promised to think about it.

Dick then said he'd do it but only if I did something for him: knowing of my background growing up in Japan and having friends in the government, he asked that I find him a certain special Japanese whiskey made by Suntory that was impossible to find in the U.S. *That'll be easy*, I thought.

Back home, I began making rounds, reaching out to the president of Suntory Japan and explaining that the former mayor of Los Angeles wanted a bottle of his special whiskey. No luck. Apparently, it was so popular in Japan that it would be months before anybody could get their hands on a bottle. Not even the president of Suntory himself could get the mayor a bottle.

Next, I tried a member of the Japanese Parliament who was very close to the Prime Minister. I hit pay dirt and, on my next trip to Japan, I tucked the special bottle of whiskey into my luggage and arrived back in Los Angeles: mission accomplished. You might say I'd sunk to a new low in my quest to make this movie: becoming an international bootlegger.

Bottle in hand, I arranged a meeting with the mayor and produced the bottle for him, reminding him of his promise. He promised to get back to me, but the $5 million never materialized and my subsequent attempts to remind him were met with steely denials from his assistant.

That wasn't the first time I'd been promised money by people who flaked on me. Where to begin? You already know about the 26-year-old fake rich girl, but there was also the fashion model from Monaco who promised me $5 million. She even signed a contract for it, but week after week she kept experiencing delays in wiring the money. She had transposed the account numbers, she said, then insisted that she had to send her personal assistant to Miami to get the monies moving.

Weeks went by. Nothing in my account. I told her I was going to go to the King of Monaco and complain to him that one of his subjects was reneging on an agreement. She ignored me. I Googled her and discovered that she'd been on trial in Finland for stealing a car from her former husband or fiancé. Signed contract or not, it was time to let this one go.

Then there was the American billionaire. One of our mutual friends strongly suggested he should invest in the film. We had several emails, and I quickly realized he'd been burned in the past by Hollywood types—something that is very common, unfortunately. During one of our email exchanges, he said he would be in but only if nobody made more than $100,000 a year. After all, he reasoned, when he helped finance Facebook, Mark Zuckerberg had only made $55,000. I was nonplussed and at a loss for how to respond.

How could I go to my actors, or many of the others involved in the movie, with those kinds of numbers? It was simply impossible. After that initial turndown, he nonetheless invited me up for a meeting. I spent the night in the city, and with my colleague John I showed up for breakfast at his home at 8 a.m. sharp. He had just injured a leg and was sporting a cast. Soon the chef prepared our meal and placed eggs Benedict in front of us. Said investor promised me $5 million, but said he needed to check in with some advisors.

In the months ahead I was ghosted.

As I sat down to dinner with Dennis and discussed the film at Gladstone's, I just focused on not blowing it by saying something that would turn him off or freak him out. I still didn't know what cooled Nic to playing the Gipper, and I didn't want to screw up this opportunity to work with Quaid.

Dennis had read the script and liked it. I shared my vision for the film and after a few hours of back and forth presented him with a replica of Reagan's cowboy hat that set me back $250 at the gift shop of the Reagan Library. He grinned and tried it on. Tapping the rim of his new hat, he promised to get back to me after he read the script one more time.

A week later I was at home when Dennis's name lit up my phone screen. I hit the Talk button and escaped to my garage. "I tried on that cowboy hat you gave me, but it's just too big—it doesn't fit," he said. My heart was in my throat as I prepared myself for yet another rejection. But he paused for dramatic effect and then added: "But I think I can grow into it."

And with that we were off. Next it was time to make an announcement.

One of my core philosophies of filmmaking is that I want to both make an excellent movie and then communicate excellently about that movie. You can't do one without the other. So, I carefully planned the announcement in two steps: First, I gave the exclusive to *The Hollywood Reporter*, which broke the story in June 2018. A month later, Dennis and I traveled with my good friend Megyn Kelly to the Reagan Ranch in Santa Barbara where we filmed a special episode of *The Today Show*.

After months of planning, Megyn arrived at the ranch and Dennis and I drove up together, him driving and me guiding him with my GPS. But the ranch is situated in an area that confused the GPS.

We soon found we were on the wrong side of the mountain, only a short distance away from the ranch but inaccessible, nonetheless. As we backtracked and rerouted, I was furiously sending Megyn text messages and even a photo of Dennis and me, profusely apologizing for keeping her waiting, hoping she didn't stomp off the set. But she wasn't like at all, welcoming us graciously as we arrived, and prepared for the taping.

At the Reagan Ranch, Megyn, Dennis, and I had time to catch up before the interview began. Once the two of them were positioned inside the small adobe where Reagan and Nancy once lived, the questioning began. She covered the gamut—asking him questions about his career, past drug use, politics, and everything else. We were in close quarters and I was impressed with her ability to temper her obvious respect and admiration for him with the courage to ask tough questions.

When they began to discuss religion, though, I was a bit nervous as they ventured into Oprah-speak, talking in a vague manner that sounded like many roads lead to heaven and God being in the flowers and the trees, or something like that.

Now it was time for my debut and the three of us walked outside toward Reagan's beloved lake with cameras rolling. I recounted the story of how I came to choose Dennis for the role and how he messed with me. We had a great time and, after we finish filming, we reconvened in downtown Santa Barbara for a late afternoon lunch. It was the first of many times I spent with Dennis. I took him to the Reagan Library and the Friends of Ronald Reagan dinner with business executives in Los Angeles where he gave a talk, and I gave the closing prayer.

As Dennis and I spent time together I quickly realized what an important part his mother Nita played in his life. I noticed many similarities between her, my mother, and Nelle Reagan. He told me how excited Nita was about him playing Ronald Reagan and how important her faith was to her. I asked him, "What kind of Christian is she?" to which he immediately replied, "You know the kind that believes the earth is six thousand years old!"

Oh, that kind!

I made plans to have Nita, and my mother live with us on the set of the movie and sent her flowers on her birthday. But alas, my plans fell apart when Nita breathed her last. She had reached the ripe old age of 92 when one day in the fall of 2019 she texted her nurse to say her heart was fluttering and felt funny, to which the nurse responded that she'd be there in five minutes. Nita's last response before quietly dozing off into eternity was "Okay."

Dennis invited me to Austin for his family's memorial service for her. She had already been laid to rest at a large funeral in Houston where she spent most of her life. But this gathering was a small, quiet affair at a church in Austin, attended by no more than seventy-five close family members— and me and my daughter Emilyn, the odd ones at the party.

Dennis was joined by his younger children, Thomas and Zoe, as well as his older son, Jack, now an up-and-coming actor. I arrived with Emilyn and headed straight to the church, arriving as Dennis was doing a rehearsal of the program. I could tell he had picked up lots of tips from directors over the years as he choreographed each speech and song.

He urged his son Thomas to speak up and stop swaying as he read Nita's favorite Bible verse, and he reminded Zoe to speak slowly. His son Jack needed little direction, and soon it was Dennis's turn to sing "On My Way to Heaven" along with a new song he wrote after Nita's passing.

As the guests filed in, Dennis followed the pastor to the stage and gave a testimony of faith in Christ, mentioning how Nita had noted in her Bible that she had become a Christian in 1947, a born-again Christian in 1982, and that Dennis seemed to be following a similar path. He looked at each of his children sitting in the front row and urged them to also find Jesus and be born again.

His was an impressive and powerful plea from a dad who knew he hadn't always walked on the righteous path. He also noted for good measure that his fiancée, Laura, and he were now putting God in the center of their relationship.

Afterward, Dennis and I, along with our kids, got into his car and headed over to his apartment where the whole group gathered on a rooftop terrace to eat and fellowship. Chatting with his aunts and uncles and hearing their stories, I could see that Dennis did indeed have much in common with Ronald Reagan—they were both from the heartland. Watching him conduct himself with his family at the service, I couldn't help but think that this was probably the way Reagan had handled his mother's memorial service in 1962.

By this time Covid had begun to impact the world and I'd been carefully following the news. This trip, as well as another leg to Hawaii to meet with an investor, were trips I almost didn't take because of safety concerns. But I was learning to take risks. And that trip was one of those risks. As we boarded the plane to leave Austin for Los Angeles and then Honolulu, I was still concerned about catching Covid and was taking appropriate precautions. Emilyn and I were slathered in hand sanitizer, and instead of staying at a hotel, we stayed with friends.

Just before I left Austin, Dennis pulled me aside and urged

me to use him to raise funds for the film. I thanked him because fundraising had been a great challenge. Although he'd been patient, it's not good for actors to be attached to projects that can't find funding.

In our case, in addition to the obviously flakey funders, we also had well-intentioned funders who just couldn't deliver what they promised. One funder, based in Canada, assured me he was in for $5 million but the money was always "around the corner" or days away. Month after month went by with nothing but empty promises.

I was particularly annoyed because I had allowed *The Hollywood Reporter* to run a story on this company funding us. Once again, everybody thought we were funded and ready to go. I began to get phone calls from people this company had worked with previously, warning us gently but firmly that while they were well intentioned, they had never come through with money before. My concern deepened.

My director Sean called me every once in a while, to warn me that actors have been know to drop out of projects when they take to long to begin. I assured him we were fine. Besides, what would he have to gain by quitting on a project that's been announced so publicly on *The Today Show* no less?

It was a few weeks later that my Google alert indicated a new story about Dennis and our movie. He had talked to a British publication and lamented that our movie wasn't going to happen.

"This is the first time I'm saying it: it's not happening," Dennis said. "I don't think they have the money. I was really looking forward to it because I got a shiver of fear up my spine about it. He was my favorite president of the 20th century . . . he was emblematic of my mother and father's generation and a great communicator. It's a really good script. I'm feeling cheated."

I was shell-shocked as I read the article on my phone. What to do now? What if my current investors saw this? Especially after I'd already paid him a good-faith deposit. It's a British paper so perhaps no one would notice. But what if it got picked up by an American publication? I called Dennis, but it went straight to voicemail. I mumbled something about how sorry I was for the delay and asked him to give me a call.

What to do next?

I called his best friend and our mutual friend Kenny. Both Kenny and Dennis's fiancée Laura had been big supporters of the film. In fact, it was Kenny who encouraged Dennis to take the role when he was trying to decide whether he should. Kenny, Dennis, and I had gone to the Reagan Ranch in Santa Barbara and that was the day, Dennis told me later, when he decided he would take on the role.

Kenny calmed my fears a bit and suggested a course of action: wire Dennis another $100,000 immediately, which would give Dennis the assurance that his project was indeed real. Kenny urged me not to say anything to Dennis but to let him handle it, and thankfully he did. A few days later, Kenny called to say that Dennis was fully on board. I'd survived what could have been a death blow.

But in those twenty-four hours of uncertainty, I did have to think through what I would do if he pulled out of the project. In addition to the actors I've already mentioned, there was Dylan McDermott, whom I'd met through a mutual friend, and told him of my interest in him playing the role. We had set a date for lunch at a favorite L.A. haunt for actors, the Soho house to discuss it.

Dylan was a very pleasant and engaging person, and we had a nice lunch discussing the possibilities. I shared my concern that one of my three main actors would say something about Reagan that would turn off his fans. I hadn't asked, and would never ask, any of my actors who they'd voted for, but I did want to make sure they had the common sense not to tick off the film's core base of fans. Dylan assured me that wouldn't be a problem, and we parted with a promise to keep in touch.

Perhaps the weirdest of all the casting conversations was the time I got a call from a number I didn't recognize. As I was driving in West L.A. one day, I answered the unknown number and heard, "Hi this is Zachary Levi." He proceeded to ask me about some property he was looking at purchasing in Texas and what I thought of it since I had shot a movie there previously. After giving him my thoughts on the place, I hesitantly asked him what he did for a living.

"I'm an actor," he said.

"Are you *that* Zachary Levi?" I asked, and he said he was. Where to begin? Before we'd made the announcement on *The Today Show* with Megyn, I'd had to keep contingency plans going. In my mind one of those contingencies was Zachary. I was impressed with his work, his charm, and his good looks. We had several mutual friends, but I never took the time to explore the idea of his involvement in the movie with him. Before I could, Dennis had confirmed that he was in, just three days before I got this strange, out-of-the-blue call from Zachary.

What could I possibly say in such a situation? I began by telling him about the project I was working on and that I was literally planning to call him but that before I could, Dennis had confirmed he was taking the role. He thanked me but I'm sure he thought it was as weird as I did. Why would the Creator of the Universe have him call me three days *after* I'd confirmed with Dennis? It made no sense.

In any event, I always felt like Zachary was where I could turn if Dennis were to bail on the project.

By the time of Nita's memorial service, things were moving. We'd settled on Oklahoma, which has a generous program offering 37% in rebate on what we spent in the state. We'd already been on a scouting trip there and found an amazing location where we might be able to shoot most of the movie–a massive Masonic Temple.

I had been introduced to the governor, Kevin Stitt, who

promised to help us in any way he could. And in the months ahead I called upon him numerous times, asking for his advice especially as Covid hit. One time, shortly before I pulled the trigger to begin production, I called him on his cellphone and asked if he would shut down our production if we began. He promised me he wouldn't, saying while other states may shut down, he wouldn't and that Covid was simply the new reality. Although adjustments would be made, he assured me shutting down the state was simply not in the cards.

I had two main investors who, by this time, had committed significant sums of money. Though their funds were in place, the final funds were needed to begin. I was still waiting for two groups who had promised $3 million each. One was a businessman who had invested a half a million dollars, but then as I pressed him for the balance of $2,500,000, he suddenly disappeared off the face of the planet. I began to think he died of Covid.

My co-producer John assured me that we had enough funds to at least complete the first part of our shoot, and the worst-case scenario was to pause and raise more funds before we proceeded to finish the film. But what about Covid? What if we were hit with unexpected expenses or shutdowns?

John called me needing a "go/no go" decision. We could punt to the following spring, or we could go for it now. But going for it now was sort of like driving in a hailstorm not knowing what comes next. I thought about it quickly and said, "Let's go for it."

I haven't always been so decisive. I still drive by the house that I could have/should have made an offer on twenty-five years ago but didn't move quickly to take the risk. I still think about the movie I was offered the lead role in when I was 14 but decided to pass. It seems my life has been full of these kinds of missed opportunities.

But this time I made the decision to roll.

And we were off for the adventure of a lifetime.

I authorized work on the construction of the Oval Office, and we began meetings in earnest to decide on members of the cast. Most were easy negotiations. Some, like the one with Jon Voight's agent, not so much. As he got more and more challenging, I had to prepare a Plan B and that was John Rhys-Davies. I'd already made the offer to John to play B.E. Kertchman, a Russian who visits Reagan's church in his youth, but now I reached out to him to see if he'd play Voight's role in case we couldn't come to terms with Jon. He seemed open to it.

Of course, I was hoping to reach a deal with Jon. He and I and this project went way, way, back. Ten years to be precise. Jon is an interesting fellow, always unpredictable, friendly, yet guarded somehow. I still haven't learned his rhythms but not for lack of trying.

Back in 2010 I had called to offer him the role of Cyrus Reaper in a film called *Doonby*. When I explained what the role was and asked if he'd be interested, he replied. "No. But how are you?"

"Well, I'm good, Jon," I said, "but are you sure I can't give you more information about this role?"

"No."

With most of our funding secure, I reached out again and reminded him that he'd previously worked with my director Sean. That did the trick. He was in, provided we could reach a deal with his team. As our people worked out terms, Jon and I began to explore in detail the character he would play. Unlike most of the characters in the movie, this one was made up, having come to me in a dream.

Once Jon learned that little detail, he quizzed me about what the character was like and then we explored it together. One of the key elements of his character was the other character he spent most of the movie sparring with, the role of the young Russian member of parliament who visited Jon's character Viktor.

For this role we kicked around many names, but it was

important to me that it be someone Jon felt good about. I suggest Shia LeBeouf, whom Jon worked with in *Holes*, but that didn't seem to excite him. He suggested an actor he had worked with on a recent series, but that actor passed on the opportunity. Then we learned of a Russian actor named Alex Sparrow and arranged for him and Jon to communicate. Before I knew it, they'd become fast friends and were working on their lines via Zoom.

26

CASTING ABOUT

Having read books about Nancy Reagan, I am aware of her power and the sheer force of her personality. She singlehandedly destroyed some careers and elevated others, depending on how she thought they were treating her husband or whether she thought they had his best interests in mind. I knew she could destroy our movie if she so chose, so one of the first communications I had early on was to let her know what I was doing.

I didn't seek her endorsement, but neither did I want her to be an enemy of the project. So, I reached out to her via her assistant, told her what I was doing, and asked for a meeting so I could brief her. I also mentioned the time I had met Ronald Reagan at his office and my being pulled over for speeding in his hometown. Her assistant Wren wrote me back:

> Hello, Mark. Well, as I thought, Mrs. Reagan is still declining requests to participate in book, movie, or similar projects. She did, however, smile at your very cute memory about meeting her husband and especially the story of your speeding ticket! I'm glad to hear that this project is in the hands of someone

who admires my hero, President Reagan, and I'll look forward
to seeing it when it's finished. Thank you for your interest in
including Mrs. Reagan in your research.

That was all I needed. I didn't have her endorsement, but
neither did I have her opposition. I truly wanted to be able to
tell viewers of the movie that this was an independent film that
wasn't beholden to anyone who would tell us what to do or say.
Although I never did meet Mrs. Reagan, I was invited to her
memorial service.

Later I became friends with John Heubusch, head of the
Reagan Library and Museum, and met with and communicated
with him regularly. John told me Mrs. Reagan simply desired
that I kept her briefed through him before making any
announcements, a perfectly reasonable request that I honored
right up until the time of her passing.

Finding the actress to play Nancy proved to be a most challenging undertaking. Early on, I had been in contact with a
wonderful actress named Janine Turner to play the role. But we
lost touch over the years. As we contemplated production, we
turned in earnest to a list of actresses including Jennifer
Garner, Amy Adams, and Rachel McAdams. Rachel was the
most puzzling of the turndowns since she seemed to really
resonate with the material. A few months later when her preg-
nancy was announced I assumed that had been the reason.

As we zeroed in on a great actress to play this role, I remembered hearing through a friend of a friend that Penelope Ann
Miller was interested, so I reached out to the friend of the
friend directly and confirmed the rumor was true. But first I
wanted to make sure that Dennis was on board with her, so I
made a date to visit with him.

As we wrapped up our time together, I told him of our
continuing search for "Mrs. Reagan" and asked him what he
thought of Penelope Ann Miller. *"Carlito's Way!"* he exclaimed,
and I knew at that moment that we had our First Lady. Soon

after, I set up a meeting for Sean and me to meet with her at her home. We arrived and were invited to her backyard to meet with her and her husband Jimmy, who served us crackers and drinks. As Sean and I talked with Penelope we quickly became comfortable with her and could see her in the role.

After the meeting Jimmy ushered us to the door and said, "So, is she getting the part?" It was vintage Jimmy, a great guy who I would grow fond of as we played golf on the set in Oklahoma. We soon made the offer to Penelope and our agents worked out the deal.

One of the many lessons I learned through the process of making this movie is the importance of a casting director. I was introduced to Jennifer Ricchiazzi, and as casting director she made an enormous contribution to the movie. She also wore the hat of a therapist, listening to my stories of working on this film and all the crazy things that would happen from time to time.

When we had a hard time finding the actress to play Jane Wyman, Reagan's first wife, it was Jennifer who suggested Mena Suvari, the star of *American Beauty*. I'm ashamed to admit I hadn't watched it but I knew she could act and has a good body of work behind her.

She read the script, and thanks to Jennifer's great suggestion, we had a match. It was Jennifer who also suggested Alex Sparrow. She was there to help me with great backup choices when my friends didn't come through despite my best efforts.

I don't think I expended as much energy on anybody as I did on Richard Dreyfuss for the role of Soviet premier Mikhail Gorbachev. I always had Richard in mind for the role and no one else. I first met him at a party in Hollywood in 2013. When I mentioned the role to him, he said he'd be interested. So, I emailed him but got no response for several years.

Finally, I figured out through a mutual friend and Richard's wife Svetlana that my emails had been going straight to his spam. Once we figured this out, Richard and I had a nice conversation about the role, after which he put his wife on the phone. She liked the idea of the movie and the role for him. But she made it clear that Richard makes his own decisions and, while she can help, it will be up to him.

Svetlana let me know that Richard's daughter was a makeup artist, so I offered to let her do his makeup. As financing took shape, Richard and I had a long conversation about the script. To my surprise, he thought the script didn't have enough religion. Further, while his mother's and his pastor's faith were clear, Reagan himself didn't show us enough of his.

I hadn't thought of it that way, but now that I considered his point, it did make some sense. I just hadn't expected that comment from Richard. The more we talked the more I sensed a number of fundamental differences in our approach to the film. After a long conversation, I offered to get Howie involved and began to rewrite the portions about Gorbachev. That's when Richard sent me this note:

> I hope I'm not butting in where my thinking is considered inappropriate but when you say "Trying to incorporate your ideas into the final draft" I hope I'm wrong that your mindset is you've got a near final draft, because my ideas were pretty radical, and I was trying to convey a rethinking of the central take on the material . . . I am encouraging you to drop the first third of the script, all the youth . . . and aim for a new idea, the two most powerful men who raised themselves above the world's cliche view of them and under scrutiny examining themselves, while those around them keep underestimating them, wanting their meeting to be a simple victory for Reagan because Gorby wasn't brave enough. If it could be a version of *My Dinner with Andre* that's a surprise, unexpected, and can be hilariously dramatic, risky, and far more emotionally involving. Don't be in a hurry, give yourselves time to think new thoughts.

He offered an interesting and compelling angle, and he had a point, but it was a completely different movie than the one I'd envisioned. Although he may deny it, it was clearly a Reagan-Gorbachev movie with a very prominent role for Dreyfuss's character. A different movie.

The question in the air, however, was whether I could make enough changes to bring Richard along and keep the first third of the film that he didn't like. I was going to try, but Howie was skeptical that we could pull it off. Howie sent me his perspective:

> Here's the thing, and I've seen it 50 times in my storied career. The Academy Award Winner wanted to engineer the movie for his purposes, and in this case on a story basis, his purposes are quite solid. But we are making a movie about the life and ultimate mission of RR, not the final professional/adult chapter. That's the crowning achievement, not the story.

> Richard is right on another movie, that's not the one we're making. As writer, I can and will guard our project first. I seriously look forward to his insights and thoughts, but what he's talking about here is another movie. And maybe a movie I will write with him. And in my usual Reaganesque deference, I won't let him. In my mind, he can help me strengthen Act 3 and RR and Gorbachev's final act in the US and USSR showdown that RR did win—on interesting character basis. But we're not re-engineering the movie on that. He can choose whatever he wants to do and be in this, and we still love him. It doesn't depend on him. Rest easy. I got your back. I got all our backs.

Howie's always had my back against dozens of attempts to change the story I'd envisioned. Still, I was determined to go as far as I could with Richard to try and meet his expectations. I reminded myself that he's a veteran—he was starring in *The*

Goodbye Girl when I was in elementary school, and he's forgotten more than I'll ever know when it comes to film. But I know something about this character and, equally important, the expectations of the audience, and I was determined to protect the story as I saw it.

There's a fundamental disconnect between flyover country and those of us who worked in Hollywood. Part of the issue was a desire for the average person to watch a somewhat linear story of Ronald Reagan that takes us from childhood to his presidency. Most biopics cover a short window in the person's life—like the *Lincoln* movie. Of course, by Hollywood standards, *Lincoln* did respectable business at the box office, and Daniel Day-Lewis's performance as America's 16th president was stunning.

But a botched marketing campaign and a lack of ideological diversity among those who made the film left tens, perhaps hundreds of millions of dollars on the table—money that could have lined the coffers of legendary director Steven Spielberg and his partners, Disney and 20th Century Fox. As I started filming *Reagan*, I was keenly aware of the mistakes the *Lincoln* team made.

The first mistake? The creative team behind this film about the president who founded the Republican party was led by blue-state heroes Steven Spielberg, screenwriter Tony Kushner, author Doris Kearns Goodwin, and Daniel Day-Lewis.

To understand the negative implications this lineup sent to Lincoln's fan base, imagine the reaction had the gay community learned that *Milk*, the biopic about one of the most beloved members of its community, was going to be directed by Clint Eastwood, star Mel Gibson, and be based on a book by David Barton, with a screenplay written by Dinesh D'Souza.

And if that lineup of blue-state heroes wasn't enough to discourage interest from red-state Lincoln fans, Mr. Spielberg directly insulted them, declaring, "The parties traded political places over the last 150 years. That in and of itself is a great story, how the Republican party went from a progressive party in 1865, and how the Democrats were represented in the picture, to the way it's just the opposite today."

Red-staters didn't miss the insult: "Did Steven Spielberg say the GOP is just like the slave-holding South?" asked Warner Todd Huston at BigHollywood.com.

Another surefire way they kept traditionalist audiences away from their movie was bad language. The makers of *Lincoln* played that card as well. According to a *Hollywood Reporter* poll, it was Lincoln's natural fan base that was most offended by cursing in movies, with a whopping 79 percent of Republicans saying that American movies feature too many four-letter words.

In an interview after the film's release, the Civil War historian and Lincoln biographer, James McPherson, who met with Spielberg and Kushner to provide background for the screenplay, noted, "Lincoln rarely if ever used profanity, and some of the dialogue calls for him to do that. I thought that was a bit jarring."

Inserting ahistorical profanity into the dialogue and attempting to tell traditionalist stories even as various cast and crew members insulted those who formed the film's natural audience may sound like bad business moves, but they're a common practice in Hollywood where I work, despite their box-office consequences.

The film's marketing campaign was equally obtuse as cast and crew members fanned out across mainstream media for appearances on *The Charlie Rose Show, Oprah*, and various NPR, MSNBC, and PBS programs, while ignoring *The O'Reilly Factor, Hannity, Huckabee, Limbaugh, Beck*, the *700 Club* (of the Christian Broadcasting Network), and other red-state favorites.

Presented with the opportunity to make a film accurately reflecting the morals of Lincoln's time instead of ours, and to develop and market the film in a manner that would appeal to all Americans, center, right, and left, Spielberg instead chose another path, one that would almost certainly see his film honored at the Oscars, but that would also forfeit big bucks in box-office receipts.

The 79 percent of Americans who, according to Gallup, make up the center-right majority of the nation showed their displeasure with *Lincoln* by voting with their feet and asking important questions: Why would moviegoers shell out money to see a picture that seems to intentionally offend their core values? Why would traditionalists pay any attention to film-makers who think their communities are beneath them and not even worth a minimum of outreach?

Lincoln's box-office numbers fell far short of their potential, showing—once again—that Hollywood still has a lot of work to do to better understand our customers. I'll make mistakes of course, but hopefully different ones—and ones that don't insult the audience.

That said, I had other mountains to climb and was determined to both protect the story and get Richard Dreyfuss on board—a possibly impossible task but one I wasn't ready to give up on yet. I enlisted my director Sean to help. When I explained the situation to him, he reminded me that actors wanted to be heard; once they feel heard, they will often come around.

I took his advice and decided we, as a team, would hear Richard out. So, John, Howie, Sean, and I jumped on a call with Richard and let him talk. For nearly an hour. He painstakingly explained his position and we listened with few interjections. To tell you the truth, we were fascinated with him and the quality of his arguments. But when we were done, I was ready to throw in the towel. I asked Howie to give it one more shot—which he spent a week dutifully doing.

I sent his revised script to Richard and held my breath. And waited. I gave our casting director Jennifer a call and asked her to tell Richard's agent we'd made all the changes we were going to make and, though we'd love to have Richard on board, it would have to be with this script. I waited some more. Finally, word came from Jennifer: Richard is out. I was disappointed beyond words, especially after seven years of working on him.

On the other hand, I couldn't sacrifice the integrity of the project for any single person. I had dreamed of an all-star cast, but God apparently had other plans. Now to go to work on the other all-stars.

Producing movies is strange. Some movies I've had almost nothing to do with, yet I received a producer credit. Others I spent years on and got no credit. *The Vessel* is an example of the former, *The Chronicles of Narnia* the latter. I learned a painful lesson on Narnia because I never received a producer credit. To be honest, I was so happy to be at the show that I didn't work to position myself to receive a proper credit.

I started working for Walden Media at the time when it was acquiring the rights to the property. I was responsible for bringing Disney in as our partner on the first two films. Yet the Disney executive I had first brought the film, Rick Dempsey, and I were increasingly pushed aside by people who couldn't have spelled Narnia the year before. We watched with disappointment as others received producer credits instead of us. I vowed that that would never happen again.

The Vessel starring Martin Sheen was one of those I didn't have a lot of involvement with creating, a film I joined as a co-executive producer after it had already been shot. It's a wonderful movie, though not one destined to be a box office hit, but nonetheless one that had heart.

Although I had made a little money on the project, it was wonderful to share producer billing with the legendary director Terrence Malick. But the project allowed me to be in contact with Martin Sheen. I had always envisioned a role for him in *Reagan*. I wanted the cast to be truly bipartisan as much as possible and so I asked Martin if he'd take on the role of Jack Warner.

After sending him the script we discussed it, and he

promised to give it some consideration. A few weeks later I received this neatly typed letter from him:

> Dear Mark, many thanks for your letter which arrived with the script *Reagan* this past week and kindly pardon my brief reply. I read the script (well written) but I simply cannot see myself as Jack Warner or any of the other possible roles available. I just want to thank you for thinking of me and wish you well with the project and, by the way, I think Dennis Quaid is perfect for the part. I know he will be extraordinary.

I was disappointed of course but had long learned to just roll with the punches and remember that the DP was guiding, even in these types of rejections. I was convinced, though, that I'd have better luck with the legendary Robert Duvall for the role of George Shultz. I visited Shultz a few times at his office at Stanford and developed a warm friendship with him. I reached out to Bob through a mutual friend, and he expressed interest and asked to see the script.

A few days later I was once again disappointed by a "No."

That began another long series of setbacks. I called him to try one last time or at least to understand the reason for his no. He blamed a busy schedule and, of course, we were in the middle of Covid. My last attempt to get him to change his mind failed.

Eventually we found a great character actor named Xander Berkeley, a man of great skill and talent who had been in several important films and series. On set I was especially pleased to learn of his progressive politics as I'd always wanted our cast to be full of people from all political persuasions.

With Dreyfuss out, Jennifer had come up with the idea of Olek Krupa, a wonderful Polish actor who was eager to work with us. Jennifer gave us miracle after miracle, including Kevin Dillon to play Jack Warner, the talented Mena Suvari to play

Reagan's first wife Jane Wyman, and the ageless Lesley-Anne Down to play Margaret Thatcher.

Although I never fancied myself a casting director and was pleased to work with someone of the caliber of Jennifer, there were several roles that I had cast myself several years earlier: these included Robert Davi, who I had always imagined as a scary Soviet leader Leonid Brezhnev, Jon Voight as Viktor, Kevin Sorbo as Reagan's preacher, and David Henrie as young Ronald Reagan.

Originally, I had Nick Jonas pegged for that role, having been introduced to him by the head of the Reagan Library, John Heubusch. Nick and I met at the old A&M lot in Hollywood to discuss his playing the role. Although we never announced him in the role, as time went on, I began to sense less and less enthusiasm on his part for the character.

He was also getting older, and I needed this character to begin at the age of eighteen or so. Another person I had considered for the role of young Reagan was Zach Efron One day as I left an LA Laker's game Zac was literally walking next to me in the tunnel leading away from the court. A mutual friend had mentioned the possibility of working together so I brought it up. He didn't respond terribly enthusiastically, and it was around this time that my friend Eduardo Verastegui, an actor and producer, told me about David Henrie. I was intrigued. He was a few years younger than the others and he seemed to have a good head on his shoulders.

In addition to finding great actors for the roles of Nancy and Ron, I was looking for actors who wouldn't cause problems for Reagan's core fans. It wasn't about politics, mind you, but more a question of what the actor might say or do publicly that could depress turnout. A *Hollywood Reporter* poll had found that 52% of Republicans skip movies where the star is a liberal while 36% of Democrats skip movies where the star is a conservative, so it was important that my lead actors playing Ron and Nancy were somewhat above politics.

Of course, I never asked them what political party they belonged to, but I needed to know the top two actors at the least wouldn't say dumb things in public that might give movie-goers a reason to stay home.

Some of those doozies include the incredibly silly comment made by Christian Bale who was starring in *Moses*. On the cusp of releasing the movie, Bale said he thought the prophet Moses was a "terrorist" and a "schizophrenic." Okay. If you say so. Clearly Bale forgot that Moses is a hero to three world religions. The audience heard his comments and stayed away.

Then there was the equally tone-deaf Jennifer Garner who, shortly before the release of her film, *Heaven Is for Real,* thought it would be a great idea to insult every Christian mom in America who was thinking about going to her movie by teaming with *Vanity Fair* to produce a video in which she delivered the punch line "Go the f— to sleep" as bedtime reading for her children.

I, too, experienced this phenomenon with *The Chronicles of Narnia* when the director, producer, and lead actor all went out of their way to say insulting and silly things aimed at conservative Christians, depressing the turnout. Our producer, when asked whether Narnia was a Christian story, responded that it was about whatever religion one wanted it to be about. Right.

Of course, the better answer would have been that the story follows the trajectory of the story of Christ but was made for people of all faiths.

I had no such concerns about my lead actors Dennis, Penelope, and Jon. Although I'd never asked them who they had voted for, I knew they didn't have contempt or hatred for those Americans who held traditional beliefs, and I had one less thing to be concerned about. Not to mention their amazing performances, which completely blew me away.

27

THE PROPHECY

I've always thought it strange that Hollywood has such a fear of honest-to-goodness portrayals of religion—if it happens to be of the garden variety Christian type. If you dropped in from outer space and watched our pop entertainment, you would think we are highly secular people since it seems that, in TV land or in most movies, nobody ever prays, goes to church on Sunday, or engages in religious practices of any kind.

Think of *I Love Lucy*. Here, an Irish woman (McGillicuddy) marries a Cuban guy (Ricardo), and yet nobody attended Catholic Mass. And that was the 1950s. That's our media. But through books I've worked on like *Rock Gets Religion* and *Pop Goes Religion*, I've advocated that our media should reflect our lives and that we shouldn't be afraid of discussing spiritual things and telling our spiritual stories to each other.

Perhaps I was shaped by my upbringing and the fact that my father was a preacher. Or perhaps it was all those *Guideposts* stories I read as a kid, the magazine that often had stories about divine encounters and how God leads in our lives. I'd be a hypocrite of the worst kind if I didn't include the spiritual aspects of how I was led to make this movie, even if the reasons may seem a little weird.

One of the reasons I insisted on financing this movie independent of the major studios was because I was keenly aware if I did allow that kind of financing, I wouldn't be able to have a final say on the content. I also knew it would mean gutting Reagan's story of the spiritual nature that was always part of it.

Kengor's book and his articles that were foundational to the story are so important because he was one of the few authors who dug deep to try to understand Reagan's spirituality. My friend Terry Mattingly, a renowned religion columnist, speaks frequently about religion being "the ghost" in many stories.

By that he means that often it is impossible to understand the motivations behind people's actions if you don't understand their faith. In that sense it is the invisible thing that moves and motivates them. For instance, how to understand Michael Jackson's obsession with being perpetually a child without understanding that the religion he grew up practicing didn't allow the celebration of birthdays and Christmas?

With Ronald Reagan I had a hunch early on that his faith was the key to understanding what he did in life and why. With the hundreds of books written about him, for the longest time only one, *Reagan Inside Out* by Bob Slosser, mentioned an important spiritual moment in Reagan's life. Slosser highlighted the time a Pentecostal preacher prophesied over Reagan that he might be President one day.

Now, my job as a storyteller isn't to pass judgment as to whether it's crazy or not, but to be faithful in telling Reagan's story in a way that explains his character. I'd say that was a key moment. It would be years before that story appeared in a more scholarly form, and that was in Kengor's book as well as articles he'd written.

What really made Paul's work stand out for me was the fact that he alone thought to go to the church that Reagan grew up in, where he asked to see the sermons young Ronald Reagan heard in church. He was told they were in the basement and that nobody had ever asked to see them before. Paul discovered a treasure trove of documents there, helping make what Reagan would eventually do visa vis the Communism, make sense. His church was visited by an anti-Communist Soviet defector, and his pastor regularly discussed the evils of Communism.

But when it came to that spooky prophecy scene, I felt we were on solid ground to include it in the film especially because I had access to the last living person who was in that scene, Pat Boone. I quizzed him many times about exactly what went down that day. Yet, those who know me know I am a critic of so-called faith-based cinema because I find it too preachy.

Art shouldn't be preachy. Still, I wanted to tell the story in a way that would let the doubters doubt and the believers believe. So, I hit upon the idea of letting one Russian atheist tell it to another Russian atheist, neither of whom believed the story.

And that's how the story was presented in the movie. On a breezy evening at his home, Reagan was wrapping up a meeting with three devout Pentecostal Christians—including Pat Boone—when one of them, a preacher named George Otis, offered to pray. As the group gathered in a circle they held hands. Otis recalled the moment:

> I was just sort of praying from the head. I was saying those things you'd expect—you know, thanking the Lord for the Reagans, their hospitality, and that sort of thing. Everything shifted from my head to the spirit—*the* Spirit. The Holy Spirit came upon me, and I knew it. In fact, I was embarrassed. There was this pulsing in my arm. And my hand—the one holding Governor Reagan's hand—was shaking.
>
> I didn't know what to do. I just didn't want this thing to be happening. I can remember that even as I was speaking, I was

working, you know, tensing my muscles and concentrating, and doing everything I could to stop that shaking. It wasn't a wild swinging or anything like that. But it was a definite, pulsing shaking. And I made a great physical effort to stop it— but I couldn't.

Otis then prayed as though it was God speaking directly to Reagan through him, saying these words: "My son, you are the ruler of a state which is the size of many nations, and I am well pleased with your labor. If you will continue to walk uprightly before Me, one day you will live at 1600 Pennsylvania Avenue."

Pat recounted it to me, word for word, and the only thing that differed each time he would tell it to me was whether Otis had said "live" or "dwell" at the White House.

What made that tale even more interesting were two subsequent stories I heard relating to it. First, one day I was visiting with a guy who told me the story of how at the moment Reagan lost the nomination to Gerald Ford in 1976 he had been at his side. Reagan had turned to him and said, "I guess it wasn't God's will."

Four years later, the night Reagan won, Boone called him and, to his surprise, Reagan answered, and Boone said that he had wanted to be the first person to congratulate him by calling him "Mr. President." He then asked if Reagan had remembered the prophecy he'd received in Boone's presence ten years earlier. "Yes, Pat, I've thought about it many times," was Reagan's cryptic response.

I was fascinated because those three stories taken together ring true about what may have motivated Reagan to pursue the highest office in the land. The first was what it was, and we are probably divided into camps of skeptics and believers of some sort. But the second seems universally probable.

At 65 years old, Reagan likely thought he lost his last shot to be President and may have wonder if he had done something to not live up to his end of the bargain in the prophecy—to live uprightly. Was that why he was not going to be President? Then four years later he confirmed for Boone that he had thought about it often.

Exactly fifty years later we re-created the prophetic scene in Guthrie, Oklahoma, at a private residence we rented to shoot the movie. Pat flew in that day and got ready to re-create the scene for us. Only this time he would be playing his friend George Otis—while Dennis and Penelope played Ron and Nancy, and an actor named Chris Massoglia played Boone.

Before we began, Sean asked Pat to tell us exactly how it went down. With cameras rolling, he recounted the story again in vivid detail. And now we were ready to shoot. Our cinematographer managed to create some spooky lighting approximating the light bouncing off a backyard pool. The scene was mesmerizing. And you, the audience, get to decide whether we pulled it off or not.

But it's very important to me that we came back from that scene immediately to the skeptical KGB agent and his Russian mentor for them to register their shared protest, namely, that the whole thing was crazy. And isn't that the beauty of faith? Things that seem illogical to one, like a man resurrecting from the dead, are articles of faith to another. There's nothing wrong with telling the story and letting each viewer reach his or her own conclusion.

Like Reagan, I had my own inexplicable prophetic moment as well. I was about seven years into the process of developing the movie, facing opposition at every turn, when I got a call from a friend who wanted to know if I'd speak to a man who prays for people. Who would turn that down? Sure, I said.

One day I jumped on a call with him as I drove through West L.A., but before he offered that prayer, he began to say a word of prophecy. Having been around church my entire life, I've learned to take such things with a grain of salt.

After all, sometimes it seems like for every normal Christian person there seem to be ten hucksters out of their religious minds. But I was open and tried to temper my skepticism that afternoon. He immediately got my attention when he began to talk about two parts of my story in making this movie—coins and Presidents. I'm spooked by what I hear. He began, saying:

> I was watching the Lord put four coins down on the table and when He turned the coins over, He told me to look at those coins. What I saw on those coins were presidents.

After adding some complimentary things about my skills, he continued:

> The Lord is trying to communicate something to me still. I walked onto a movie set, and on that movie set I was watching a transition with an actor that was assigned and there was a transition. And He has given you an anointing to break forth in new ways and step forward in places that are going to open this next season for you.

> The Lord says that these hurdles you jump get higher. Each one you will overcome and, because you are steadfast and obedient, you are able to jump over those hurdles . . . because you have jumped over these hurdles you have found a place to run forward.

> It is a season of running and God says you are going to run with a new endurance, with a new perseverance in a way that you have never been able to before.

I won't bore you with the rest of it, but you get the idea. Everything was spot on to the point that I asked him if he had Googled me or the movie. He said he hadn't, and he had no idea even who I was. My pastor is skeptical of these kinds of things and calls them "Christian voodoo." Still, in my darkest hours when it appeared as if the movie would never happen,

I'd remember these words from a man I didn't know and then keep marching forward.

I shared this encounter with almost nobody, remembering what was said about Mary when she received the prophecy from the angel Gabriel, namely, that she had "kept those things in her heart," as opposed to blabbing about them to the neighbors. But I did share it with Howie the screenwriter who wrote back:

So, I have to give you my own prophecy moment—when I hung up the phone with you two weeks ago after this other guy demanded you fit his budget number regardless what you had to cut, and hearing the weariness in your voice as we racked our brains on how to do it . . . knowing in my heart it was impossible.

Your vision and the burden you were given could never be wrought in the earthly realm for that, and you knew it. You'd make it, but for the rest of your life, you'd regret it. I prayed then and there for strength for you, and that the right person would come along, and see it exactly as you described this individual seeing it—that is all matters. All of it. And God's treasure would flow.

This story and this man are so important, and we know in our guts this land is hanging in the balance at the edge of a slippery slope. This is probably your life's signature profession and ministry, and perhaps country-saving moment, and as you put it, it's the hill you'll die on. That's how you wrangled me in —the chance to do what we're doing. Most importantly my first prayer got answered.

You're strong and convicted again. I can hear it in your voice. I pray that this is The One, and that this is the Moment we've been working and praying for. But even if it's not, I hope you see it as I do . . . we're not crazy, man, we are driven. We're in this fight for life . . .And we keep swinging. This is going to happen. Congrats. I will remain in prayer and remain ready to leap back in when we get The Call.

That's Howie: always faithful. The man who took the vision and wrote it into reality, all the while incorporating my ideas along the way. Who could ask for anything more from a screen-writer and a friend?

Along the way I learned one more interesting thing about Reagan's faith. It was at once both hidden and out in the open. It was deep, but not easily apparent to all. And as I dug deep into this side of who he was, I came across a fascinating story recounted by John Morris, who once headed up the Ronald W. Reagan Society. Morris wrote:

Ronald Reagan's yearbook picture in the 1932 Eureka College Prizm is accompanied by the following mysterious statement: "The time never lies heavily upon him; it is impossible for him to be alone." Having seen this quote countless times on display in the Reagan Museum on campus, never had its meaning been understood to me before. I would inquire with others as well, but nobody seemed to be able to make sense of it.

Considering so much else of what the Great Communicator said and wrote throughout his life made perfect sense, why would Ronald Reagan presumably have chosen such an obscure and mysterious quote for his yearbook entry? Perhaps this was a rare exception, a fluke, a hurried attempt to say something smart before the deadline passed for submissions?

But as Morris dug deeper, he came across an article that appeared in a publication called *The Spectator*, where Reagan got the quote.

There is another kind of virtue that may find employment for those retired hours in which we are altogether left to ourselves and destitute of company and conversation. I mean that intercourse and communication which every reasonable creature ought to maintain with the great Author of his being. The man who lives under a habitual sense of the Divine Presence keeps up a perpetual cheerfulness of temper, and enjoys every moment the satisfaction of thinking himself in company with his dearest and best of friends.

The time never lies heavy upon him; it is impossible for him to be alone. His thoughts and passions are the most busied at such hours when those of other men are the most inactive. He no sooner steps out of the world but his heart burns with devotion, swells with hope, and triumphs in the consciousness of that presence which everywhere surrounds him; or, on the contrary, pours out its fears, its sorrows, its apprehensions, to the great Supporter of its existence.

Morris concluded:

These eight decades after he chose this quote, it seems to me that this passage represented yet another gift of wisdom from Ronald Reagan. What more beautiful example for the young leaders could Ronald Reagan have given than the contemplation of this mysterious quote?

All leaders will face loneliness. Next time you are feeling alone, give a thought to Ronald Reagan's yearbook. "Live under a habitual sense of the Divine Presence . . . it is impossible for him to be alone."

Indeed, I can say from experience those are words to live by.

28

MARCHING TO GUTHRIE

For the longest time we planned to shoot the movie in Georgia, since it has great tax incentives that lure many filmmakers there. Several states have enacted incentives over the years giving filmmakers a rebate on all monies spent in their state, once certain qualifications have been met. I made a trip to Georgia in 2013, scouting out locations including the Pinewood Studios built by Dan Cathy of Chick-fil-A fame. Now renamed Trilith, Cathy's team created quite an impressive campus.

But Oklahoma also loomed large in my mind as it had instituted a rather attractive rebate program. In late 2019, I made a trip there to meet with some businessmen, as well as the governor and his cabinet, to scout out a particularly interesting property, the Masonic Temple of Guthrie, Oklahoma.

My co-producer John had filmed there before and saw it as a strong option. As we made our way up the steps of that massive building, I noticed it resembled the U.S. Supreme Court and realized we could shoot almost the entire movie at this incredible location. There were long hallways where we could re-create the opening scene with Viktor, auditoriums with stages that could house the Oval Office, and any number of smaller rooms where scenes could be staged. It was perfect.

Heading back to Los Angeles to celebrate Christmas with my family, I could see that things were taking shape. Within a few months of that visit, we were preparing to leave for Guthrie.

As I readied the family for our two-day sojourn to Oklahoma from Los Angeles, all I could think about was the million things that could go wrong. Not only was I moving seven people and a dog across the country, I was also diving headfirst into the unknown—like making a movie in the time of Covid, risking my investors' money, and knowing full well I could be shut down, forced to go back to Los Angeles at any moment.

Before we left, I spent several weeks with my two youngest children, swimming and frolicking with them in the pool, trying to take my mind off the incredible stress that wanted to consume me. People think kids are a cause of stress, and perhaps sometimes they are. For me, they're just the opposite: they're stress relievers, helping me to take my mind off my circumstances when I spend time diving into their world of fun.

"Play is the work of children," I sometimes tell them, and I spent much of the summer of 2020 in the water, mentally preparing for the journey ahead.

As we set out in the RV, we made our way to New Mexico that first night and landed at an Embassy Suites. Covid travel was bizarre and the next morning at breakfast, the buffet was gone, replaced by individual servings and things wrapped in plastic. As we crossed state lines into Oklahoma, we suddenly heard a loud bang, followed by lots of little bangs. I pulled over to the side of the road, and Kara and I decided to go on the roof to see what was happening. We quickly discovered that an awning had come off and a large metal pole was flopping around. A massive wind continued to cause it to flail about.

I volunteered to try and pull it up so we could grab hold of it. I sprawled out on the top of the RV and lifted the pole up. But as I did, it suddenly flew up and over my head and landed on top of the RV. A split second later, I heard Kara scream as I've never heard her scream before.

The pole hit her with massive force. Surveying the scene, I simply couldn't figure out why she wasn't knocked out or onto the pavement on the other side. She could easily have died here, I thought, leaving my kids without a mother. As we climbed down together, I was amazed at how we were protected, but I couldn't help but wonder if this was an omen of things to come.

We made arrangements to stay at a ranch owned by a friend, and as we got close, the rain was coming down in torrents. It was difficult to see ahead. What was supposed to be three cabins was now two, which I had to cram nine people into —my family plus the two assistants who had joined us for the trip. And did I mention that there was no Wi-Fi for my Zoom school kids? In short, the first few days were nothing short of a nightmare. But there was more bad news to come.

As I worked to find us housing closer to where we'd be shooting the movie, I got the disheartening word from my production team that one of the unions had informed our actors they were shutting the movie down because of various "issues" with our paperwork. I won't bore you with the details, but it had to do with a large amount of money we didn't have that they were demanding that we escrow.

I called my attorney and asked him if he had ever seen such a case before, to which he replied that he hadn't. This deadlock went on for several days as I faced the real possibility of having my movie shut down before it had even started. One of our team members had started a prayer group comprised of those who had committed to pray for the movie, and he quickly informed them, asking for their prayers.

With the prayers of those seventy-five people behind us, a combination of threats and compromises from our lawyers settled the matter and we were now ready to begin shooting.

Shooting a movie during a pandemic is truly a surreal experience like no other. Part of the fun of making a movie is the joy of being together—of going to restaurants and local haunts, and generally hanging out with cast and crew. When I first landed, I went straight to our Covid Coordinator and asked her what the rules were for my stay there. The conversation went like this:

"Can I go to a restaurant?"

"No."

"What about Walmart?"

"That's absolutely the most dangerous place of all."

"How am I supposed to eat?" I asked.

She just stared at me.

Eventually we made a plan, and Walmart groceries were delivered to my door daily. We were living in a rental—my 92-year-old mother, my wife, my kids, a caregiver, and an assistant. While I was off at work, the kids were doing Zoom school, and we were trying hard to make normal out of chaos. At least there was a jacuzzi in the backyard.

I arrived at the old Masonic Temple in Guthrie and got a tour of the place—seeing where we'd be shooting various scenes—and then we drove over to our office located on the third floor of a prominent building in downtown Guthrie. Before we settle in for meetings, I decided to take a stroll around downtown. As a light rain began, I grabbed a poncho and tried to get my bearings.

There were plenty of signs around describing the kind of town Guthrie once was: lots of pubs, references to it being a place of refuge during Prohibition, and the quiet bitterness that comes when your town used to be the capital of the state but for some reason isn't anymore.

I walked past the railroad tracks and noticed a dilapidated old bus with shrubbery growing all around it. I saw a scene that reminded me of the album cover of my friend Dan's band Jars of Clay and decided to send him a picture of it. I walked the streets quite a bit during this shoot. Somehow it brought me peace to walk through town, focusing and praying as I gave my stress to God who knows everything about everything.

I'm mindful of my high school friend Dorleen, who wrote this insight as her senior quote in our school yearbook: "Every night I turn my problems over to God . . . He's going to be up all night anyway."

Back in Guthrie, we began a series of meetings with our team and I was encouraged that the whole gang was beginning to take shape and form a family of sorts. Howie, Ronald Reagan personified, arrived. Always optimistic, always cheerleading, the man who could easily have given up many times but remained relentlessly upbeat.

John, on the other hand, was the realist—ready to tamp down any excessive optimism while Sean shared Howie's overall outlook and a cheerful determination to shoot every scene possible, even if it meant breaking the budget. A typical pattern in our conversations featured Sean arguing for a scene, John saying we can't afford it, Sean saying we can go find the money, and me saying we don't want to get money from people who are invariably going to use our need as leverage against us.

Ah, the financiers. I could write an entire book on some of the folks I've encountered from that world. I've experienced them all. In addition to the woman who pretended her dad owned a hedge fund instead of a Kinko's and the Finnish woman from the outskirts of Monaco, there was the man who pretended to be a billionaire, but who, upon getting drunk one night, finally spilled the beans that at the most he could personally invest only a hundred thousand dollars. All of which is fine, until it became clear that he didn't think I could produce my own movie and was determined to wrest control of the film away from me and bring in another producer.

I called and asked my friend Dave what I should do. "Run, don't walk away from this guy," he counseled. And I did. Dave was there from the beginning, back in 2006 or so. We were meeting in Orange County at an internet start-up where I was working at the time, and Dave swore God told him in that first moment that he wasn't there for the start-up but to meet me and help me. What an enthusiastic friend he proved to be. Always cheering me and the project on.

Then there was the guy with businesses allegedly situated all throughout South America who promised me $2.5 million and wanted to join us on the set, but then cancelled because his 104-year-old aunt died.

Then he promised he had wired the funds, but they never arrived. Then he said he would fly in with the check and asked me how long the runway in Guthrie was. Satisfied that it sufficed for his plane, he promised to fly in with the check.

He never did.

And who could forget the wealthy scion from Pennsylvania who strung me along for a year before it became clear that he didn't control his family's resources? So, you can see why it was difficult for me to allow shooting to begin knowing that we didn't quite have enough money to finish. But we began anyway.

As I set foot in our Oval Office, located on the stage of a large auditorium, it became clear this thing was finally happening. It was awe-inspiring. Built to exact specifications, I stared for a few minutes at the set before I sat in the President's chair and let the photographer take a picture of me with my arms outstretched. Later I would get photos of my son Jordan peeking through the little door in the desk, as JFK's son had once done. It was a moment to take in all that had happened before thinking again about all that could go wrong.

When Dennis arrived, we spent some important time in his trailer preparing for the job ahead, and then moved to a table read in the Dominion House—a hotel that had once been an orphanage. I stared at it thinking of all the sadness that had emanated from it, but now we were redeeming it. I felt the same way about the Masonic Temple.

I really don't have a handle on Masonry; there are those

who swear it's completely innocent and community minded, and there are those who see a dark and sinister side. I had no idea, and no clue as to what had gone on in the walls of the Temple we were shooting our movie in, I just knew that the Masons we had dealt with in Guthrie were stand up people who had bent over backwards to make our shoot successful.

But for good measure, my family and I drove around it seven times, with each family member taking a turn to pray that God's blessing would be upon it as we filmed.

Our first day of shooting featured Dennis in the Oval Office in a scene with the great Mark Moses, whom I loved watching on *Mad Men*. He was the guy with the dog Chauncy of course. Mark played Judge Clark for us and the first scene featured the response to the assassination attempt upon the Pope. Truth be told, of the dozens of movies I've worked on, I've tried to avoid being on set as much as possible. But on this movie, I felt I had to be there. So, I was on the set for nearly every moment, making sure everything was just right.

I owed this to my investors and to Ronald Reagan.

On the first day of shooting, Dennis was intense. But also, restless. If I wasn't mindful, he could leave the set and saunter back to his trailer, and when we were ready to resume shooting, his delay in reappearing could cost us precious time and money. I quickly realized that one of my important jobs on set was to keep him in good spirits, so I regaled him with my favorite jokes and one-liners. I was also showing scenes via text to Dana Rohrabacher, who was among those who knew Reagan best, and he came back to me with this note: "Right now, Dennis is playing Reagan from the mouth, tell him he needs to play him from the chest."

I relayed that piece of information to Sean, who then passed it on to Dennis because I didn't want to interfere in the director-actor relationship. Most of the time I gave performance notes to Sean instead of to Dennis directly, but there was one occasion when I pulled Dennis aside when I thought he was trying too hard to be Reagan.

"Dennis," I said. "Don't be afraid to just be Dennis Quaid." I had fought hard to get Dennis for this role and I wanted him to remember to let his natural juices flow, that God had prepared him for sixty-six years for this moment.

It was time for him to shine.

During the last three years Dennis and I developed a rapport. I wouldn't say it was always an easy rapport, but we understood each other better. He knew I wasn't a flake, and that I was delivering on all the things he needed to make the movie of our lives. And I saw how committed he was to the project and had taken some career risks to take this on. And we were marching together, as to war. We shared a spiritual bond, knit together by our like-minded mothers, mothers of sons who remained, at sixty-seven and fifty-three, eager to make them proud.

I had also seen tremendous growth in Dennis's personal life especially after he met his wife to be Laura. When I first met Laura, they had just begun dating and I was taken aback by her beauty, her sharp mind and her devout spirituality. In fact, I was so impressed with her and so sure she was going to be Dennis's wife that I inputted her contact information into my phone and put Quaid after her first name instead of Savoie.

I was very clear with Dennis that he should not let her get away. In time, they were married and there were many times over the course of the next several years that I was grateful to have her in his life as she strongly supported our movie and kept him grounded, especially as we shot in Oklahoma under such stressful conditions.

One day after finishing shooting the famous "Tear down this wall" scene, I brought Dennis over to meet my mother as she sat with a face mask on, one hundred feet or so from the dais where Dennis had just been. She stooped over in her chair as they hugged and, in that moment, I remembered that she and Dennis' mom Nita were the very reasons we were even here.

The day before we started shooting, I had invited Dennis and his wife Laura out to the ranch we were staying at for a barbecue. At the end of the evening, I asked Mom to say a prayer.

Here's what she prayed:

Continue to lead and guide and direct. You know all the things that this group faces in the days ahead. We pray that You will iron out all the problems that will face them and make a big difference in their lives, especially as they work together. Keep them in the Word of God. Keep them on their knees and on the floor, and as they work together be everything they need. Lead them, guide them, direct them, and show them the way that they should walk.

We're facing so many problems these days all around. We just couldn't imagine a time like this a few years ago and yet here we are today facing more things even. But You are in charge, You're the ruler of the Universe, and we ask You to take charge of each one who is working on this movie. Lead them in the days ahead. We praise You and worship You and honor You in Jesus' name, Amen.

Dennis and I prayed together for strength several times on the set and did a devotional with my friend and pastor Michael Guido. One day in his trailer I noticed his Bible was on his table. In the weeks ahead as we experienced setback after setback, it would quickly become clear why we needed all those prayers.

One night, on a particularly stressful day, I had awakened at around 3 a.m. and briefly found my brain reminding itself of all the problems that I would face the next morning. I remembered thinking these thoughts: *Should I be stressed about this?*

Nah . . . , and then I rolled back to sleep and didn't wake until morning.

These are the types of moments when those who follow God credit Him with giving them that intangible feeling, sometimes called "the peace that passes all understanding." I felt that inexplainable peace from time to time as we shot. Once, when I told Dennis about that experience, he remarked that he, too, had felt the same way, that we were being carried during difficult periods by a Higher Power who was giving us the strength and guidance that my mother had prayed for.

We encountered plenty of difficulties along the way. Pacing up and down the sidewalk outside of our rental, trying to coordinate various details, I was filled with the sense that I had been—and would continue to experience, these difficulties.

Sure enough, one day as John walked toward me, I sensed that something was wrong, and my intuition was right. We had our first case of Covid, but the news got worse: it was our makeup artist, the one who spent time in our talents' faces, the most dangerous person on the set in terms of affecting my main talent. My thoughts swirled. What would happen next?

We would have to shut down for ten days, but what if Dennis or Penelope or any of the others got it? This could be a fatal blow, shutting down the entire movie for God knows how long, maybe forever. Scott, our amazing makeup artist, was quickly isolated in a cottage, and we waited for Dennis's and Penelope's test results as the entire production was shut down. We brought in a new makeup artist and fortunately, because they tested negative, we were able to resume work after ten days.

But then came the difficult task of managing the news about our delay and making sure it was portrayed accurately, not blown out of proportion. As Providence would have it, a reporter from *Newsweek* was on set that day and his reporting accurately portrayed our situation as a delay, not a total shutdown. I was amazed at what could have happened and what did, and we resumed shooting with new makeup artists who would be with us until Scott was able to safely resume working some weeks later.

I made good use of our unexpected days off. One day I took our youngest two children to the Oklahoma City Zoo and rode horses with them. I had long made it a practice to take one of my kids with me on all of my business trips and joked that was to keep Dad out of trouble—and it's mostly a joke, but maybe not totally. Traveling with my kids keeps me connected to them and we get good one-on-one time on the road.

If I could go back and do one thing differently from childhood, it would be to spend some time with my dad on his travels—the lonely miles he traveled as a preacher to people in far-flung places. But of course, I was too busy. I had school and baseball and basketball and friends and girlfriends. But it wouldn't have killed me to take one trip with him.

We resumed shooting and I alternated between my RV, which served as my headquarters, and the massive Masonic Temple building. Step by step, day by day, scene by scene, the film took shape. As I watched the dailies, I was floored by what we were creating and how amazing filmmaking truly is; there's something magical in re-creating scenes from fifty and a hundred years ago; to first imagine what was said and then bring those scenes to life with people whom you admire.

It's no wonder why people are attracted to moviemaking and why we are often willing to work so hard for so little earthly reward, but instead I chose this life of uncertainty all for the joy of creating and telling stories. Each year for most of the last thirty, I'd enter the New Year asking God, "How are You going to do it this year?" Meaning how was He going to help me pay my bills? Year after year He somehow would.

Each movie I've worked on has one person or sometimes a few who are going to make most of the money, and we all know that reality going in. This may come as a surprise, but we're okay with that. For most of the movies I've worked on, I've earned a salary but most of the profits go to someone else.

On this one, the roles were reversed. I'm grateful to each person on the set for the contribution they've made. The grips, the sound guy, the camera operator, our director of photography, the caterer—they all worked their hearts out, as I have on other films, to bring *Reagan* to life, and I'm deeply grateful.

On the set, both miracles and near misses continued to happen, and I rolled with them all. One day, as we prepared for a scene in the Cabinet Room, and Dennis began to recite his dialogue, I suddenly realized that he had the wrong lines.

Somehow Howie had substituted lines without my realizing it. I scrambled to call up an old script on my phone and then showed it to Dennis who, without missing a beat, read my iPhone and then effortlessly dove into the scene as though he'd read it a thousand times.

I was simply amazed.

Some time later, at three in the morning, we had an important scene to shoot but Penelope was exhausted and in tears; we simply had reached the end of our capabilities that day. So, we called it a day and regrouped the next morning, picking up where we left off.

Penelope could be challenging to work with but only because she was always pushing us to make her character better and more like the real Nancy Reagan. She read books, watched videos, and talked to those who knew Nancy. She nailed the character as few would have taken the time to do.

Dennis and I found moments of inspiration and often riffed off each other. After a first take of the 1984 debate prep scene, I pulled him aside and mentioned that Reagan's favorite line from the movie *The Sound of Music*, which he references in debate prep, is "When God closes a door He opens a window."

In the next take, as Dennis comes off the stage after an aide suggests he watch the film, he, as Reagan, replied, "Well, when God closes a door, He opens a window doesn't He." Brilliant, I thought. I hadn't exactly suggested he do that, but I'm glad he did.

As I stood with him on the dais for the Berlin Wall speech, we reviewed the script together and he asked me for a copy of the entire speech. As we looked it over together, we both suddenly noticed an entire section of the speech we had completely overlooked before—a section devoted to Reagan discussing how each day the sign of the cross would form on a certain tower that the East German authorities could never erase.

We instantly and simultaneously realized we must include it because it is ultimately what the film is about: the power of the human spirit to overcome obstacles, and the power of the Unseen hand of a Divine Light that will guide us all to freedom if we let it.

As each day went by, a steady stream of some of Hollywood's best showed up in Guthrie. There was Dan Lauria, star of a show that I adored, *The Wonder Years*, who played Tip O'Neill for me.

I still laugh when I think of the moment he and Dennis were arguing about the psalm they were supposed to repeat together in the hospital scene they shared immediately after the assassination attempt on Reagan. Dan had recited the psalm as "Yea, though I walk through the shadow of the valley of death."

Dennis corrected him: "No, it's the valley of the shadow of death."

"No," Dan responded, "I don't think that's right."

They went back and forth a few times before I responded that Dennis was indeed correct, and we all had a good laugh as they finally got the lines right.

Even though Dan is a bit of a self-confessed lapsed Catholic, he gave me a great gift when he showed up for the scene with his rosary beads in his hands. Of course! How had we missed that? Obviously, a Catholic like Tip O'Neill would have had his rosary beads with him. Those were the moments where the joy of working with true professionals manifested itself.

Kevin Dillon, Lesley-Anne Down, Mena Suvari, and so many other outstanding actors and actresses graced our set, and, without exception, they were a delight to work with. But we were always fighting our invisible enemy—Covid. It struck again as we were wrapping up shooting Dennis and Penelope, resulting in another ten-day shutdown.

Our medical professionals thought Covid hit us the day we were shooting the aftermath of the assassination attempt; we were working in a medical clinic with very low ceilings and too many people inside.

As we wrapped Dennis and Penelope, the three of us and our spouses sat outdoors at the Dominion House to enjoy a final dinner together. By now, I think we all knew we had done something very special, and we savored the last minutes before we would go our separate ways. Penelope and Dennis headed home the next morning, and I stayed behind to welcome our next group of actors.

The next day Jon Voight arrived, and I tracked him down at the nondescript house he was staying at a few blocks from our set. We decided to go for a walk together from the house to the set. At least that was the plan. Somehow, we got horribly lost. We came upon some young kids playing in a backyard and said hello. How strange my life is, I thought— To go from defying my strict upbringing by watching a forbidden movie starring Jon, *The Champ*, at a movie theater, to roaming the streets of Oklahoma with him forty-two years later.

Talk about following the river where it takes you. I can honestly say I never once thought I would be a movie producer growing up. A fireman, yes. A baseball player, yes. A DJ, yes. A TV anchor, yes. But a movie producer? It never crossed my mind. When I landed at Walden's music division in 2000, I had no idea they would shut it down and ask me to join the film team.

Even then, I never gave a thought to producing a movie. It would have sounded like too much work to me. But step by step, the DP, as Reagan and Clark would have called it, unfolded, and now I found myself as a producer on my twelfth film, but this one was one where I carried a great deal of the weight on my shoulders.

Although I had my capable co-producer John who masterfully handled so many of the details, the ultimate responsibility was on me as the owner of the company that owned the film, and I was keenly aware that it was I who would bear the blame for any problems. On the first day of shooting, as I surveyed the landscape, which included hundreds upon hundreds of workers and dozens of trailers, the fact that I was ultimately responsible was daunting.

I learned a long time ago, when I had my twin daughters to be exact, an important Bible lesson: Don't look down. When Jesus' disciple Peter looked up, he found himself walking on water. He only began to sink when he looked down and saw the impossibility of what he was doing. So, too, I have done difficult things in life by not looking down; this was one of those times. When things got rough, I refused to look down because I knew I would sink.

After Jon arrived, we went into our second ten-day lockdown and I asked him if he wanted to go back to Los Angeles, but he decided to stay in Guthrie. I, on the other hand, felt it was time to head home. I had a family, my mother, and two assistants. It simply didn't make sense to hunker down for ten more days, and I didn't feel I was as needed for Jon's scenes as I had been for the rest of the movie.

So, I made plans to drive back—just in the nick of time, for a day after we left, all hell broke loose in Guthrie. The weather turned dark and ice storms lashed the area, resulting in electricity going out and people being unable to leave their homes.

As we made our way back to Los Angeles, I relied instead on the dailies and kept track of Jon's work at the end of each day. Just as I had hoped, he was masterful.

But I had little time to reflect on what had just transpired, for it was now time for me to focus on our next shoot at the Reagan Library and Rancho del Cielo, known as the Reagan Ranch. Since no feature film had ever been allowed to shoot at either location, it was an honor to be allowed to shoot there. I had carefully cultivated a strong relationship with both the Ranch and the Library over the course of a decade, and as we made final arrangements to film at both, that work bore fruit. We decided to shoot after the holidays.

My advance team had scouted both locations, and when I arrived at the Reagan Library, they had opened the main floor to us, something that would have been impossible had Covid not suspended all their operations. We would spend the day at three major locations: on Marine One, the presidential helicopter; on Air Force One; and the inside of an aircraft that would serve as the Korean airliner that was shot down by the Soviets.

For this part of the shoot, I was able to get several of my longtime friends into a few scenes. First, my longtime pal, Rick Chase, was something of an aspiring actor who had chosen missionary service in Japan instead. On this shoot he served as a secret service agent along with my best friend, Shin Domen, with whom I had been classmates since kindergarten. He too played a secret service agent, flying in from Hawaii to be on set.

For the flight attendant on the doomed airliner, I could think of nobody more appropriate than Kimi Evans, whom I had coached when she was on the eighth-grade basketball team during my senior year. Kimi's mother had been a flight attendant and Kimi had been KABC's LA meteorologist. She was a natural and did a great job for me. I also relied on my daughters Anna and Maryn and my wife Kara to play White House aides on Air Force One.

It was a long day, but Dennis and Penelope had turned in powerful performances, especially in a pivotal scene where Penelope, as Nancy, urged her husband to fight back against his political enemies. It is perhaps the most important scene in the film in terms of the character arc of Reagan because it's the moment he comes to a crossroads where he must change if he is to grow. Every movie follows a journey of growth; in Reagan's case this is the pivotal moment when he chooses one path over another.

As I explored Reagan's character, it occurred to me that he had two powerful women in his life who, when it came to human nature, had very different points of view. One could only take him so far on his journey, and he then needed the other to complete it. It was Nelle Reagan, with her hopeful and optimistic spirit, who launched Ronald Reagan, but it was Nancy with her skeptical view of human nature who would help him complete his journey.

Someone, it may have been Reagan's son Ron, joked that without Nancy, Ronald Reagan would have been the host of the television show *Unsolved Mysteries* instead of President of the United States. There may have been some truth to that.

But the moment on Air Force One when Nancy urged him to fight back is a transforming moment, when Reagan's habit of looking for the best in people gave way to a need to fight and expect the worst from others. It's fundamentally the pivotal scene when he went from being Nelle's boy to Nancy's and, not coincidentally, around the time he walked away from Mikhail Gorbachev at the Reykjavik Summit.

Although no slouch when it came to being tough, Reagan had a history of being snookered by his political opponents. In 1967 he had naively signed the therapeutic abortion bill that legalized abortion in California only if a woman's health was compromised. Reagan had taken his opponents at their word, only to watch as "health" was twisted to mean almost anything, which effectively legalized the procedure.

In 1986 as President, he signed a liberal immigration bill into law that legalized three million illegal immigrants in exchange for border security, the latter which never happened. It was that kind of naivete, expecting his opponents to honor their words in such deals, that left Reagan, usually a tough negotiator, weakened at such key moments.

And it was likely the reason that one of his aides, Lyn Nofziger, had to say to Reagan just before he left to meet Gorbachev in Reykjavik, Iceland, "Mr. President, I'm here because there's a lot of people worried that you're going to go to Reykjavik and give away the store."

"Linwood, I don't want you ever to worry about that," Reagan replied. "I still have the scars on my back from when I fought the Communists in Hollywood."

We had given Nofziger's line to Japanese Prime Minister Nakasone in the film, but it was the lead-up to the critical moment when Reagan moved beyond the hopeful naivete of Nelle, and embraced the realism of Nancy, that would lead to Reagan's walking away from the negotiating table when Gorbachev refused to budge on his demand that Reagan give up the Strategic Defense Initiative in order to reach a deal.

"I don't know what else I could have done," said Gorbachev as Reagan headed for his car.

"You could have said yes," Reagan retorted. And with that, Reagan, who had always said a half a loaf was better than none, left with no loaf at all. But he had grown as a man and a leader. It was on Air Force One, now parked in Simi Valley, California, that his fiery scene with Nancy came to life.

As we arrived at the Reagan Ranch, the hillsides were dotted with trailers of all sizes, and our camera crews were in place for the first scenes. Before it got too busy, I decided to go for a walk by myself away from our crew. I walked out to the pond and looked up at the hillsides that surrounded his tiny adobe. This was the culmination of a very long journey.

I had first come up here a decade earlier and many times in

between. Dennis had said in an interview that it was coming to the ranch that had helped him make the decision to take on the role of Ronald Reagan. I think we both felt his spirit when we set foot on the property, somehow cheering us on.

But there were many disappointments that took place at the Reagan Ranch as well. I had brought David James Elliott up here, and even had taken photos with him before the big blowup between him and John Avildsen. So many false starts. And now we were on location getting ready to shoot the film's culminating scene when Reagan would go on his last horse ride after the Alzheimer's diagnosis.

I had always seen that as the final scene of the film despite the many people along the way who tried to talk me out of it. Spending time with John Barletta, the Secret Service agent who would take the last ride, had only solidified that feeling. John and I joked about who should play him—Brad Pitt, I had once needled him, and we had made the offer initially to Chris Pratt.

As I often do, as our agent made the offer through official channels, I had also made a backdoor approach through Pratt's brother, who was a friend of a friend of the project. Word got back to us that Pratt was passing because of his having a newborn at home. Who really knows if the offer ever got to him. Nevertheless, we were so fortunate to have Trevor Donovan take the role.

There's another way in which the ranch has the spirit of Ronald Reagan: the way it's positioned. What made this project particularly challenging was the fact that even to his own biographer, Reagan was inscrutably hard to "get to," much like the ranch was hard to get to. Getting there was said to have annoyed Queen Elizabeth, who purportedly was none too pleased with the winding roads and the fog. When you exit the freeway, it's a good half hour or so of winding roads before you get to the gate of the property.

I'm certainly not the first person to observe that the property is about as hard to get to physically as Ronald Reagan was to get to emotionally. And maybe that's the way he liked it. Yet once you entered the gate and drove a quarter of a mile, you suddenly descended upon the most idyllic scene you can imagine, making the drive worthwhile.

I suppose in some sense we do choose to live in homes and properties that reflect our personalities, and this one certainly reflected his. In total number of days, Reagan spent a year of his eight-year presidency at this serene spot, and it is amazing to think that, as he managed one crisis after another, he did so from this completely peaceful spot.

In a few hours a hundred or so people would descend on this location—actors, camera operators, craft services, and assorted crew members, all helping us to get the scene right and give the movie the ending I had always imagined it would have.

First, we shot a couple of scenes of Ron and Nancy in the house and then the two of them taking a boat ride. On day two we began shooting the pivotal final scenes, when Barletta comes upon Reagan holding a miniature White House he has rescued from a fish tank. Dennis played the scene masterfully.

Then it was on to the scene where Barletta approached Reagan at Nancy's request, telling him that he really shouldn't ride horses anymore because of the danger presented by the onset of Alzheimer's. We did several takes and once again Dennis captured the emotion perfectly, as did Trevor.

And with that, we were off to the final scene of Dennis as Reagan taking the last horse ride. The sky was perfectly blue and, as the camera crew got into place, Dennis and I huddled in a van to stay warm, preparing for the grand finale. With all the pieces in place, Dennis mounted his horse and he and Trevor began to ride.

Sensing a special moment, Trevor and Dennis chatted for a moment as they rode, and then Trevor paused, allowing Dennis to ride off on his own as he reached the ridge overlooking the Pacific Ocean.

I had earlier asked Dennis to record the goodbye letter and I played it on my iPhone, which I held up to my ear as he rode off into the distance. It was the perfect ending to the film, but it took a lot of effort to get it, for it was one of dozens of key moments in the film that many well-meaning people had tried to take out along the way.

I knew from the moment I heard the story from John Barletta that this was the way to end the movie. I never had any doubts about that fact. This is the great challenge of independent filmmaking—to know when to stick to your guns and ignore the input of others, and when to listen and adjust. I've always looked at the process as "may the best ideas win."

I also had the great advantage of watching up close as Mel Gibson stuck to his vision for *The Passion of The Christ*, carefully balancing that vision with new information and input from others. It's a tricky and delicate balance that few achieve perfectly.

I have a mental picture of how *not* to do this: Imagine Rembrandt painting a bit then looking over his shoulder and asking for advice on what stroke he should paint next. What I saw with Mel, on the other hand, was that he shot the film he wanted to shoot and then opened things up for hundreds, perhaps thousands of people to provide input after screening the film.

He would typically show the film to a group of a dozen or so, huddled around a table in his conference room of his fourth story office in Santa Monica. As the lights came up, Mel would saunter in and ask what people thought. The reactions ranged from an old preacher named Harald Bredesen who shouted "hallelujah!" to others who had suggestions on how he could make it better.

One of my favorite moments was when a prominent preacher named Chuck Smith came in and Mel asked him what he thought of it. "I will support it, but it was a very, very violent movie," Smith said.

"Yeah, it was a real s—t sandwich, wasn't it," Mel said to Smith's horror. It was classic Mel. Then there was the time a pastor kept badgering Mel about his biblical source for his decision to give Satan a child.

"I just pulled it out of my a—," he retorted.

But other times he listened carefully and made changes. I believe it was the founder of the Christian ministry Focus on the Family, James Dobson, who first watched a cut of the film that ended with Mary cradling her dead son, staring at the camera with a "You killed him" look on her face.

Jesus, Dobson reminded Mel, had a unique story having been resurrected, and the film really needed that. To his credit, Mel went back and shot the resurrection scene, and that was just one of many changes he made when he realized that he had some blind spots, being so close to the work.

Watching our director on the *The Chronicles of Narnia* resisting attempts to keep the film from straying too far away from what C.S. Lewis had in mind, along with the director of *Amazing Grace* bragging about de-religiousizing the material, made me wary of directors with a "my way or the highway" type of attitude.

Those experiences gave me both the confidence and the humility to take a bold course, but then be open to tweaking that vision. It was a delicate balancing act that I hoped to achieve with *Reagan*.

All these things were on my mind as I boarded a plane to Oklahoma again with my wife and kids in tow to shoot the final six days of the movie. Because of having to shut down two separate times for ten days each, we ran out of time to shoot the all-important lifeguard scenes featuring young Ronald Reagan.

We had to wait until the weather warmed up. It was the middle of July when we touched down, and the humidity was off the charts. We settled into an apartment in downtown Guthrie and my thoughts drifted to the week ahead.

We'd spend a couple of days at the river filming Reagan lifeguarding, followed by a couple of days at his church when young Reagan and his mother deliver a reading, and then as they meet his pastor and the Soviet defector who visited his church. Then we were going to shoot Dennis Quaid for one day in front of a replica of the Washington Hilton Hotel as he faces an assassin's bullet.

The search for the actors who would portray Jack, Nelle, and Mugs, Reagan's childhood sweetheart, had been challenging and had taken me up to the last possible moment. For Nelle, we looked at several actresses. The week before we were to start the shoot, we offered the role to Carrie Underwood and then to Kimberly Williams-Paisley. Neither seemed to want to travel during Covid.

With only days to go, Jennifer sent us a list of a dozen actresses. As I carefully studied each one, one of them jumped out at me: Amanda Righetti. I read interviews in which she talked about being from a large family in Utah, and then quickly added she was not Mormon. She has a solid body of work behind her on shows like *The Mentalist* and *The O.C.,* and as I suggested her to the others, everybody was positive, so we made our offer, and she accepted. Soon I was on the phone with her discussing the character and was feeling good about our choice.

For the character of Jack, Dennis' agent Darren suggested a client of his named Justin Chatwin. I decided to call him and, to my surprise, learned he has a history of alcoholism in his family. It was clear right away that he had some ideas about the character and a desire to make him a more compelling one. Justin immediately sensed the script was too kind to Jack Reagan, making him a lovable drunk.

Reality, Justin told me, was usually very different. Children of alcoholics are often on edge, unable to relax because they're unsure what will set Dad off next. He wanted to work with Howie to toughen up the character a bit—something I wholeheartedly supported. Over and over, Justin told me how grateful he was that I allowed him to tweak the character.

"Are you crazy?" I told him. Letting an actor bring their experiences to the role is a complete no-brainer for both me and Sean, and we've done it repeatedly with our actors.

Penelope Ann Miller had asked for extensive re-writes, sometimes inserting herself into scenes where Nancy wasn't, not out of a sense of wanting to be an annoyance, but because of a deep desire to get the character right for the good of the movie. I was thrilled with the performances we were getting out of each of the characters, and Justin and Amanda were just the latest in a string of actors who were taking the movie to the next level.

After setting up shop in our apartment in Guthrie, I had some time to gather my thoughts. I began by going for long walks around the town, remembering when I first scouted out the place and then again during our shoot a year earlier. After we were shut down by Covid for a second time the previous fall and we had finished our shoot and returned to L.A., I felt sometimes as though I had PTSD. But now I was looking forward to finishing strong.

As I walked, I came upon our assassination scene. The Washington Hilton Hotel wall near the spot where Reagan almost lost his life was perfectly re-created by our design team. The next day Dennis was in front of the wall reenacting the amazing moment and we were off to the races.

Dennis had a long day that began with that scene and then moved to a variety of pickups including a talk with his aging mother Nelle who was played by an old friend of mine, Jennifer O'Neill. The scene was a beautiful one that found 40-year-old Reagan telling his mom he's washed up, divorced, and feeling lost.

As Dennis and I discussed this scene, he said he wanted to change some of the lines. I asked him if he had a similar conversation with his mom and he quickly said yes, around the time he and Meg Ryan were getting a divorce. "Let's just riff off that," I told him, and he did so brilliantly, telling Jennifer's character Nelle that he hasn't lived a perfect life in Hollywood and that maybe he can't do the great things she told him he was going to do someday.

I had put in the script a line that my mother had said to me hundreds of times, growing up: "Remember Whose you are and Whom you serve," which Nelle repeated to her son. All these years I had thought it was one of my mother's originals, but a Google search revealed she'd picked it up from a devotional writer named Oswald Chambers.

When it came time for Jennifer to deliver the line, she told me it didn't sound grammatically correct. I assured her it was and that seemed to reassure her, and she delivered the line perfectly.

We moved on to the final scene of the night and Dennis's last of our shoot, when Reagan was in Las Vegas. This was the moment when Reagan was at the end of his rope, smoking a cigarette and drinking a beer, as voices from his promising past swirled around in his head. The scene culminated with him throwing the beer bottle against a wall backstage at the show he was forced to perform to pay his mortgage.

It was a scene we had crafted carefully. I had called up his old friend Pat Boone and asked him: If Reagan was down and out in Vegas, how low could he go? Would he have reached for the bottle? Would he have thrown it across the room?

I had posed the same question to a Reagan biographer who had assured me that Reagan would have done no such thing and that Reagan had specifically said of the Vegas show that it was difficult but still part of God's plan for him.

Pat would have none of it, and we went with his note. Even if Reagan later saw it as part of the DP, in the moment it would have been a huge disappointment, and yes, he might have taken a drink and lost his cool. So that's how we played it.

It was near midnight when we finished, and as Dennis

walked down the stairs, we hugged one last time. We had been on a long, arduous journey, through countless peaks and valleys, and now we were nearly finished with the shoot.

The next day we shot David Henrie as young Reagan. David had patiently waited after we announced him in 2015 or so, and now he was ready for his closeup. He had meticulously worked up Reagan's Midwest accent and delivered it brilliantly as a life-guard at the Rock River, and then as he traveled the streets of Iowa looking for a radio job.

Then it was on to his scenes with Jack and Nelle. Finally, it came time for the scenes of young Dutch, portrayed by an actor named Tommy Ragen who had starred in another movie for Sean, *Mighty Oak*.

As Justin and Amanda wrapped up the final scenes, we had one last moment together as cast and crew and I thanked each for their contribution, and with that, the show was over. Shortly after we finished, I received this most gracious text from Amanda: "I just made it home and wanted to thank you again for trusting Nelle to me. I am humbled and grateful for the opportunity and experience. Thank you from my heart."

29

LIKE A RIVER

Making a movie is like riding a bronco or, better yet, following a winding river. You can fight the river, or you can roll with it, letting it take you where it wants to take you, even as you work hard to keep from capsizing. A great deal of my time guiding this movie was spent resisting dumb ideas and recognizing great ones when they showed up unexpectedly, ideas that helped the story take shape.

I've always known the movie needed to begin with the Bible verse II Chronicles 7:14. Not because it was important to me or anyone making the film but because it was important to Nelle Reagan.

When her 69-year-old son had taken the oath of office for the most powerful position in the world, he had placed his hand on her Bible, specifically on that verse—the verse next to which she had scrawled in the margins: "A wonderful verse for the healing of a nation."

The verse may have been misappropriated lately by some, but that doesn't change the power of the wisdom in that verse for us. I had always seen it being repeated by 11-year-old Ronald

Reagan who often publicly recited poetry and Bible readings with his mother.

The verse, well known to Christians and Jews, reads, "If my people which are called by My name, will humble themselves and pray and seek My face and turn from their wicked ways then I will hear from heaven, forgive their sins and heal their land."

Of course, the most amateur of Bible scholars will tell you that this verse is God speaking to ancient Israel, but it also applies to any people who consider themselves to be His people, which means it can apply to any of us. And the promise is for any nation as much as it is for America.

It's a good reminder to all of us, and what makes it especially meaningful is that it doesn't single out specific sins but leaves that up to each of us to figure out based on our own conscience and the laws laid out by God in the Bible. When you think of it that way, we all have sins that we can repent of.

I'll never forget the last time I saw Judge Clark. He was in a wheelchair at dinner, and when I approached him to say hello, he asked how the project was coming along, indicating that he was praying for it. I don't recall what else we said to each other, but I remember looking back at him as I walked away, seeing a look of knowing in his eyes, as though he was communicating to me that it may be a long road ahead, but with the DP it would all work out.

I wish I could say that I always knew it was going to work out, but that would be a faith-based lie. The truth is that even the most devout among us never know if the DP includes our plans coming to fruition. I've had so many dreams that died despite my belief in the DP, and I've had to learn the hard way that the DP may not be my plan.

Then there is the matter of God being outside of time and space. Nineteen years may seem like a long time for a dream to become reality, but for Him, existing outside of our timelines, it may be like a minute or two.

Sure, I contemplated what success might look like, but I also imagined failure. I thought of this as I sat down to have lunch with my first investor.

In my nightmare scenarios in which everything fell apart, I would have to go to him and apologize for losing his money. But on this day, as we ordered off the menus of his swank private club in Palm Desert, it was a celebration of sorts as I shared with them that we were going to begin shooting shortly. I felt the same way for the others who had believed in me along the way and invested their hard-earned money in the project.

Somewhere in the middle of the process of bringing the film to life I saw that I had a few things eerily in common with the main character. I'm not a famous actor, but I do have a Bible thumper for a mother, and although my father wasn't an alcoholic, he was publicly imperfect in our community, and I felt the son-of-an-alcoholic type pressures to do better than he had.

And just as Reagan read a book at the age of eleven and a half that helped him become who he was supposed to become, I also found a book, at the age of 12, that helped give me a role model—a book titled *Sincerely, Ronald Reagan*.

I saw Dennis working out issues from his life in this movie. He told me of the time he was driving down the highway with his dad as they listened to "The Speech," as it's come to be known—the 1964 speech Reagan gave on behalf of Barry Goldwater that effectively launched his career. I noticed on set that he had some scenes with Jane Wyman's character Mena Suvari that were eerily reminiscent of what Dennis encountered with his then-wife Meg Ryan whose career had skyrocketed, as Wyman's had, eclipsing their husbands' careers.

I saw it too in Jon Voight as he regaled me with stories of the time he visited Russia with his mother, who approached President Boris Yeltsin and asked him if she could have the pin he was wearing. In our movie, Jon plays a Soviet agent who worked closely with the Soviet leadership.

Then there is my co-producer John who sometimes let it

escape that his father was an alcoholic, not unlike Jack. John is an amazing man of character, but I sometimes got glimpses of trauma that may have been related to his dad. He too was probably working out his own story with this movie as he sought to be a better dad than his was, to his two daughters.

We told each other stories to make sense of our lives and our experiences, and to better understand them, and yes, to avoid making the same mistakes we saw our elders make. At this 1984 debate Reagan said, "It was Seneca, or it was Cicero who said, 'if it was not for the elders correcting the mistakes of the youngers there would be no state.'" I suppose that's true. It's also true that "tradition is the democracy of the dead."

I don't know what heaven is like, but if you knew my father, you would clearly see that the last four years since his passing have found him angrily arguing with God to please fund his kid's movie. Perhaps he was joined by Nelle and Jack and Reagan himself. Who can say how these things work?

My father was a staunch anti-Communist as Reagan was, and his political activities sometimes put him in conflict with the generally apolitical community I grew up in. He would attend anti-communist meetings, and I noticed that he spoke of Reagan early on as though he was a Johnny-come-lately to the cause, sometimes mispronouncing his name as "Reegen" intentionally as though he wanted to make it clear that he had junior status in their movement against Marxism.

After I met President Reagan in 1997 and realized that his office was seeking visitors in order to keep Reagan active and stimulated, I began to introduce others. I got my cousin Pam in to see him and then my oh-so-serious father-in-law, Daryl, who said upon meeting the President: "I've respected you for many years," to which Reagan responded without batting an eye: "I've been expecting you, too!"

But when it came time to get my father in to say hello, I was informed that he had flunked the Secret Service background check. Although I had no concrete evidence, I'm pretty sure it was due to his political activities, which included crazy exploits like sending hot air balloons from Hong Kong carrying Bibles into China.

I'm often asked why I wanted to tell Reagan's story. It's simple really.

We need stories of those who have gone before us to help us navigate life. When he was 11 years old Ronald Reagan was given a book called *That Printer of Udell's* by his mother. The book helped him become who he was supposed to become, and without it, he may never have reached his potential. The hero of the story, Dick Falkner, was the son of an alcoholic who found faith in God and grew up to become a United States Senator.

Young Reagan went to his mother after he finished the book and said, "I want to declare my faith and be baptized. I want to be like that man." And he did. And that's what stories do for all of us in one way or another. When we stop telling our stories faithfully and truthfully to each other, something within us that is precious dies.

Some critics might attack us for making this film because we don't hate the character Ronald Reagan, and thus, they may think, we may try to glorify him. But anybody who knows me knows that I would never allow that to happen.

As Dennis has so eloquently said, when he comes to play a character like Reagan, he has to quickly get over the admiration stuff because the character, knowing his faults, doesn't admire himself that much. He knows he came from dust and to dust he will return.

And besides, a story about Superman without Clark Kent just isn't that interesting. If nothing is at stake and everything is perfect, there's no drama or tension, both of which are needed to tell a great story.

The Bible is maybe the best example of storytelling in this regard, for its allegedly heroic characters are presented, flaws and all, and the truth is, if Christianity and Judaism were made-up religions designed to win converts, they would never have allowed their holy books to be so full of great men and women who were so incredibly flawed.

Just as the Bible shows David sleeping with his neighbor's wife after ordering a hit on her husband or Moses killing a man, so our movie shows Reagan going against his own stated principles in dealing with Iran during the Iran-Contra Affair and making any number of mistakes. It's all a part of what makes the character human.

Ronald Reagan may have been "inscrutable" to his official biographer Edmund Morris, but I've never felt that was the case. And, after meeting and talking with dozens of those who knew him well-as well as meeting the man himself, and pouring all of that into the film, I hoped you've been able to understand him better with this movie. If so, then the journey was well worth it.

30

THE ENDGAME

After completing our shooting, I knew we were just beginning.

Now it was time to begin the long and arduous process of screening across the country. If I have a trade secret, it is this one—something I learned from watching Mel Gibson during *The Passion of The Christ*. I traveled to eleven states, screening for three thousand people during the three years we were in the editing process. Almost without fail, after I finished a screening, I called my editor Clayton to share my notes with him.

It's this process that helped me understand several key things to incorporate into the movie. First, I learned from the audience that we had made the fatal assumption that everyone understood why the Evil Empire was evil. How could I have missed this? How could we all have missed this? We made the film assuming everyone knew why the Evil Empire was evil, but for people under 40 that was not a given.

Typically, I screened at our office where we have nine seats and, after the film plays, I ask questions. I do the same on the road for larger audiences. Looking potential viewers in the eyes and hearing their questions and concerns is invaluable for me. In addition to young people not understanding why Communism is evil, there are other issues: Initially, we didn't meet Dennis Quaid until about twenty-five minutes into the film.

But my viewers were restless. They came to see Dennis Quaid playing Reagan—but where was he? They were also very clear about which characters they cared and didn't care about. When it came to the women in Reagan's life, they cared about Nancy, they cared about Nelle, they cared somewhat about Jane Wyman, but they simply didn't have the emotional bandwidth to care about his teenage crush, Mugs Cleaver.

That's too bad because I loved the story of her breaking up with him, but the audience just didn't respond well to her.

That's just a sampling of what we learned in those screenings, but they led to real changes in the very structure of the film. Instead of moving through Reagan's life in a completely linear fashion, I moved most of the childhood to flashbacks, and instead of beginning with his childhood, I began with the assassination attempt.

And to emphasize how evil the Evil Empire was, we created an entire opening sequence that showed some of the horrors of life in the Soviet Union. As we made these and other changes, I could see the changes in the audience's reaction. There were fewer and fewer objections and more and more tears.

I knew we were on the right track.

Opinions also differed from city to city. At a screening in Silicon Valley, there were cheers during the section where Reagan discussed tax cuts. At a screening in Nashville there were cheers during the Evil Empire speech. It seemed that each city had a unique response based on the parts of the film that most spoke to them.

Even though most film critics panned or outright avoided reviewing the movie, we eventually scored a 98% rating at Rotten Tomatoes from those who watched the film, and I believe that was a direct result of these many screenings.

31

MUSIC

As any filmgoer will tell you, music can make or break a picture. I knew this would be especially true of this movie. When our movie was announced in the press, I began to get dozens of solicitations from composers who wanted to work with us. But when it came to a composer, I wanted to defer to my director Sean.

He had a favorite candidate, John Coda, a childhood friend who had also provided the score for several of Sean's films. So, I had a meeting with John. I really appreciated his love for the subject and his sensibilities overall, so I rolled the dice and brought him on board.

But perhaps the most challenging part of our musical journey was securing artists to sing in the film and on a separate collection of songs I was putting together, songs inspired by the film. Early on I had compiled a list of sixty or so artists I wanted either in the film or in that "Inspired By" collection. If you were to have asked me which artists on that list would be the most difficult for me wrangle, without missing a beat I would have replied "Bob Dylan and KISS."

Irony of ironies, they turned out to be two of the ones who came on board.

I had reached out to Bob early on, exchanging messages that were passed on to him by his manager. At first it was merely logistics—trying to find a time when he wasn't on the road to screen for him. But after nearly two years of going back and forth, we finally reached an impasse, and it seemed like we just couldn't make it work. But through a series of communications, we were able to get to "yes" and now the only thing left to decide was what song.

Early on I had made it clear that we'd be open to any song he'd like to write, and the plan was to have him write an original composition. But over time he suggested the idea of covering a classic. His first suggestion was the Gene Autry song "Boots & Saddles." Sounded interesting to me. But when we attempted to clear the publishing rights, we struck out.

Bob had another suggestion: "Don't Fence Me In," by Cole Porter. I loved that idea, as it spoke to Reagan's life, and the fact that Bob had obviously given this some thought made it even more appealing. We were able to quickly clear the publishing rights, and Bob was able to record the track. Before long, the track was in my inbox. I still remember where I was the first time I heard it—a special moment indeed. I will forever be grateful to Bob for giving me the song, and I hope to collaborate again soon.

Even as I was being turned down by lesser-known artists, I was once again surprised, this time by the founder and leader of the band KISS, Gene Simmons. Through a mutual friend I met Gene and invited him to screen the film at our studio. As I sat with Gene watching the film in our screening room, I was reminded what a strange life I lived.

As young Ronald Reagan read a Bible verse on the screen in front of us, and as the ending later brought tears to Gene's eyes, I was reminded that this was the very man I had heard about in the fundamentalist Christian circles I grew up in, the ringleader of a band that stood for either Knights or Kings in Satan's Service.

Obviously, Gene wasn't then—and isn't now—a Satanist of any sort, but that was his reputation. And yet the Gene I met on this day was gracious and sincere and eager to discuss a collaboration. But the collaboration I had in mind was quite different from what he had in mind.

A few days later I called him and asked if he'd contribute a KISS song for the "Inspired By" soundtrack. Gene threw me the curveball of all curveballs: He wanted to do a cover of the Charlie Chaplin–penned song "Smile," but with a twist: "I'd be willing to do a version of the above, using only strings, in the style of 'Yesterday' by the Beatles."

Gene continued, "The reason for that is that music has become compartmentalized. Hip-hop over there. Country over there. Rock over there. If you can get a song in a style that appeals to the masses, it would do you good. That's my thought for today."

It was an intriguing idea of course, but completely out of left field. And the idea for the "Inspired By" soundtrack was to have the artists write songs after they'd watched the film, but how often do I have an opportunity like this? Once again, we were unable to get permission from the owner of the song and were back to the drawing board. Gene had another suggestion: "Stormy Weather." This time it cleared easily, and we set about to find the right spot for it in the film itself. But where?

John had a great idea—the nightclub scene when Ron and Jane break up. So, after working up the track in Nashville, Gene and I were soon in the studio in L.A. recording his vocals. I brought along my son, Jordan, who knows nothing about KISS or Gene Simmons, and he listened intently as Gene and I discussed the vocal and began to record. But not before Gene and I engaged in a vigorous discussion of religion.

I was amazed at his knowledge of the history of the Bible, and though neither of us convinced the other about our views, we had a great banter. As we placed the song in the scene, it fit perfectly as though it were meant to be, the DP perhaps, sung by a man who has been demonized by the religious community for decades now, but one whom I am most thankful to have crossed paths with and grateful to call friend.

Finding the ending song, however, was proving to be a much more difficult task. Our placeholder had always been "Desperado" by the Eagles, but I was dubious that we were going to get permission from the man who once wrote disdainfully of Reagan in his song "End of the Innocence," Don Henley.

My favorite was "Landslide" by Fleetwood Mac, and we also had the option of using an instrumental piece. And at one point we had thought of Dylan's "Don't Fence Me In," but as we closed in on our release date, we had a big decision to make and it rested with me, ultimately.

Dennis was not in favor of "Don't Fence Me In" for the finale and neither was John. I took their opinions seriously. But it *was* Bob Dylan, and the song was amazing. I needed an expert opinion. Someone who loved Bob Dylan as I do, but also understood film. So, I called my college classmate Scott Derrickson, the director of *Dr. Strange* among other films, and explained my predicament.

Scott obviously saw the importance of having a song by Bob, but also the necessity of making sure the final song packs the emotional punch that is needed as Reagan rides off into the sunset and into his greatest weakness—the onset of Alzheimer's disease. Scott urged me to follow the emotion first, and that meant moving "Don't Fence Me In," to the credits and finding another, more emotional song for the last horse ride.

For a brief moment Dennis and I toyed with the idea of using AI to have Johnny Cash sing *Desperado* and we even came up with a version that we both liked. Ultimately, that idea was quashed by members of Cash's family.

John had a favorite that was pushing for a while: "Country

Roads" by John Denver but covered by someone else. At this point the easiest thing to do was to just let John Coda's instrumental piece which he lovingly crafted play as Reagan rides off. But that would be the safe route. Why play it safe?

I decided to reach out to country legend Clint Black who readily agreed to take a crack at "Roads" and, a few days later, he sent over his version. However, it was a little too upbeat for our purposes. With some creative editing on the part of several members of our team, we created a more dramatic and emotional version of the song, beginning with some female vocals and ending with Clint.

We'd finally nailed it, and we were proud of the way the film ended. Finally.

I had been working on this movie so long that people have begun to die on me. B.J. Thomas is one such case. Andrae Crouch is another. Back in 2015 when I told him what I was working on, B.J. sent me a demo of an amazing song that I loved, "Walls Will Fall (Love Remains)."

As for Andrae, one day we were in his studio and I noticed that among the mediocre new songs he was playing was a stunner, something about his mother. "That song is amazing," I told him, urging him to allow me to record it for posterity's sake. But he demurred.

Finally, he agreed and tried but broke down crying halfway through. Somehow, I was able to get him to try one time through. He was aware of the movie I was making, so I hung on to the song for the "Inspired By" soundtrack. As we neared the finish line, I noticed that we were going to have a hole in the credits after the Dylan song, so I plugged in B.J.'s song and it fit perfectly.

Other songs soon fell into place, with the help of my amazing music supervisor, Tim Cook. We wanted Genesis's song "Land of Confusion" for a section of the film devoted to anti-Reagan protesters. When Tim approached management they declined, saying they were not fans of Reagan. Exactly,

Tim countered. That's why they should give us the song because it amplifies all the hatred against Reagan at that time. So, we got the song.

"Wild Thing" by The Troggs was another favorite. Imagine my surprise when I learned that the song was written by Jon Voight's brother, and Jon helped us obtain the "friends and family rate."

I needed a song from the time period to play around the time that the Berlin Wall fell, and I couldn't think of a better song than Guns N' Roses classic "Sweet Child O' Mine," and I couldn't think of who better to call on to play the guitar riff that Slash made famous than my friend Phil Keaggy—considered by some to be the greatest guitar player in the world. Phil quickly agreed and turned in a masterful performance that married the intensity of the original with the creative flair that characterizes Phil's work.

There are two other musical performances in the movie that we had to record, since they appeared in the film lip-synching: Moriah Smallbone and Scott Stapp. Much has been made in the press of Stapp being in the film, with speculation over why he was chosen.

The truth is I had planned for several of my rock friends to appear in the film: Alice Cooper, Dave Mustaine and Gary Cherone—I imagined them playing Soviet generals sitting around the table in the Kremlin—but when the time came all three weren't able to make it, with Alice catching Covid, Gary dealing with the death of Eddie Van Halen, and a scheduling mix-up with Dave, but Stapp did, and now it was time to record that Sinatra song "Wish on a Star."

Finally, I called upon Robert Davi, my actor who capably played Soviet leader Brezhnev and has done entire albums devoted to the Sinatra songbook, to sing two Sinatra songs, "Nancy with the Laughing Face" and "This Town."

32

THE FINALE

As we screened the film for the major distributors, we had lots of takers but none who were willing to put the marketing money that we wanted behind it to release it in theaters. Not only were they risk averse, but they also simply didn't see the audience that we saw. Thus, they were willing to release it, but not risk their own funds to market it.

But one day my friend Lee Roy Mitchell, the founder and owner of Cinemark Theaters, told me I should talk to his son who was launching his own film company. Lee Roy and I go back over ten years, and he would often tell me that if I got the film made, he would make sure his company would come alongside it.

Before long Kevin and I had worked out a deal to bring *REAGAN* to the big screen. We settled on a date: August 30, 2024.

Both Dennis and I had sworn that we didn't want to release the film in an election year, but here we were, delayed by the actor's strike, Covid, and even the war in Ukraine. For better or worse, our film would release right in the middle of an election season. Ugh. But once again, I had to defer to the DP. I had purposely avoided political overtones in the film, and as we tested both Democrat and Republican audiences, we found that both sides reacted well and didn't feel it was too political.

As we neared judgment day, we threw a grand party at the premiere, held at the world-famous Chinese Theater in Hollywood. And what a night it was. My assistant Louis surprised me with a hotel room that was so large it had in fact once been the rooftop restaurant of the hotel.

The next day, many of our stars and other celebrities descended on the theater and we partied until the wee hours of the following day.

On opening weekend, the numbers started coming in, and we ended up #3 at the box office, but more than doubled the number that had been predicted by box office professionals. I was pleased. And as for the critics, well, let's just say they weren't enthused, giving the film a combined 18% at Rotten Tomatoes, contrasted with the 98% from those who didn't criticize films for a living.

It wasn't a surprising number as I don't make films for critics but for the audience, and most of the criticism seemed to focus on Reagan and not even our movie. Still, I was able to turn those lemons into lemonade by getting the story into the media that we were now officially the film with the highest gap between fans and critics, an 80-point gap, besting the previous champion, which only had a 65% gap.

I even came up with a tagline we used in the campaign, posting a dozen of the nastiest quotes from reviewers alongside the words "With all this hate it must be great."

It had been a long and arduous journey, but my work and the work of my amazing team was now on the big screen with small screens to follow, for ages to come. I was glad it was over but knew there were many more challenges ahead. When my friends asked me what I was going to do next, I replied that was sort of like a husband asking his wife, as she was giving birth, how many more children they could have together. Like that poor woman, I just couldn't think of such things at the moment, but perhaps in six months or a year.

The famed producer Laura Ziskin once said, "Movies aren't made, they are forced into existence." I couldn't agree more. But they're also guided by the DP, if one believes in such things. And I do. The film may not be Divine—at least according to the critics—but I go along with the notion that each of us has something in life that we are supposed to do, and with Divine help and guidance, we can achieve it.

It may be something the world considers great, or something small. It may be rearing children, discovering the cure for cancer, digging ditches, or playing the piano, but we all have a destiny and a purpose for being on the planet, if we'll look and listen for it and work to reach it.

ALSO BY MARK JOSEPH

The Lion, The Professor & The Movies: Narnia's Journey To The Big Screen

Rock Gets Religion

The Rock & Roll Rebellion

Faith, God and Rock & Roll